CON

OF LIFE

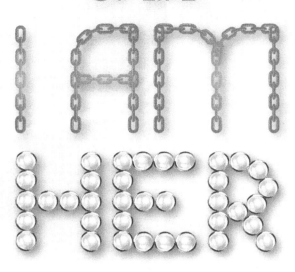

Women of the
Bible Anthology

CONVERSATIONS OF LIFE

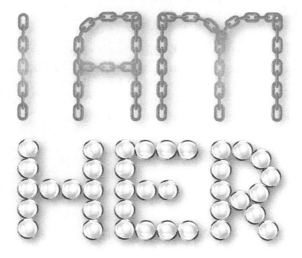

I AM HER

Women of the Bible Anthology

Nycholle Woolfolk-Gater
including 11 Contributing Writers

HUNTER ENTERTAINMENT NETWORK

Colorado Springs, Colorado

To order products, or for any other correspondence:

Hunter Entertainment Network
Colorado Springs, Colorado 80840
www.hunter-ent-net.com
Tel. (253) 906-2160
E-mail: contact@hunter-entertainment.com
Or reach us on Facebook at: Hunter Entertainment Network
"Offering God's Heart to a Dying World"

This book and all other Hunter Entertainment Network™ Hunter Heart Publishing™, and Hunter Heart Kids™ books are available at Christian bookstores and distributors worldwide.

Chief Editor: Deborah G. Hunter
Book cover design: Phil Coles Independent Design
Layout & logos: Exousia Marketing Group www.exousiamg.com

ISBN: 9798859173518 (Hardcover)
ISBN: 9798862483482 (Paperback)

Printed in the United States of America.

Dedication

I dedicate this book to my husband, Darrick E. Gater, who recognized me through the eyes of Ruth, a caregiver. You opened my eyes to Ruth in a way I had never considered. Also, as your Proverbs 31 Wife, you recognized I had ten talents, and you helped me to cultivate all ten. Thank you for the countless mornings of stealing your Spotify account, so I could play praise and worship songs for *Conversations of Life*. You really are a man of God, thank you.

To Brittany and Amber, my modern-day HER's. I am grateful for the time I get to share with you and the beauty of watching my daughters parent. You make me proud to be your mother.

To Tessa, my granddaughter, at the age of four, you taught me how to respectfully decline the things I don't love. You are a present-day, Deborah.

To each author, thank you for partnering with me. To each reader, I thank you.

Acknowledgments

To the present-day Ruth, Hannah, Sarah, Huldah, Esther, Vashti... *Her* story is waiting to be written, and one day, you will write it. The day you write it is the day you will see *Her* because you are *Her*, **We are Her.**

Until then, may the blessings of the Lord be upon you!

"I AM HER"

Dear Lord, I pray that everyone who delves into this anthology may come to know You as their Lord and Savior. I beseech You to use the study of Your daughters, the Women of the Bible, as depicted through the lives of the women in this anthology, to bring healing to those women who are suffering and enlightenment to the men who may not fully grasp the gift they have in a woman.

I implore You to perform a new work in the lives of Your daughters, so that every eye may witness, every ear may hear, and every heart may embrace Your Word with joy. I earnestly pray that every woman ensnared in bondage and chained by sin may experience a "sudden" release from the shackles of captivity.

Heavenly Father, touch each and every reader and meet them through the stories of the Women in the Bible. Illuminate the scriptures, allowing Your Word to quiet the clamor and distractions of life, if only for a moment, to perform a new work in their lives. I pray for revolution and restoration.

Lastly, Lord, I petition You to raise up present-day Deborahs, Sarahs, Esthers, Marys, and Marthas across the world. "I AM HER" is a testament to the impact of sisterhood and the transformative power of knowing who you are. Through this anthology, the voices of these remarkable women merge with the voices of those who embraced the journey together, igniting a guiding light of inspiration for generations to come.

Are you ready to join this remarkable sisterhood, replace the chains with God's pearls of wisdom, and be part of a legacy of empowerment and faith? Discover "I AM HER" and let the revelation of *Her* loose the chains and replace them with the wisdom of pearls for your soul. The Word of the Lord says, *"And suddenly there was a great earthquake so that the foundations of the prison were shaken; and immediately all the doors were opened, and everyone's bands were loosed"* (Acts 16:20, AMP). Amen!

Table of Contents

Introduction

Picture this, the year 2005; I am unable to sleep. Afraid that if I sleep, I won't wake up and my final destination, hell.

I left church again, cursing my husband in the parking lot. Yep, I can't even explain where all this "righteous anger" comes from. I quoted Paul so many times that even I was sick of hearing it. For what I want to do, I do not, but what I hate, I do scripture,

"For I do not understand my own actions [I am baffled and bewildered by them]. I do not practice what I want to do, but I am doing the very thing I hate [and yielding to my human nature, my worldliness-my sinful capacity]" (Romans 7:15,KJV).

At this point, I am sick of the scripture, so I know the Lord must be sick of me reciting it. I was exhausted, but this night was different. I didn't simply ask for forgiveness; I wanted answers. I was demanding that the God who knows the very hairs on my head would help me to understand why it is that I do what I don't want to do. Why didn't I have self-control, self-awareness, or self-regulation? How can I begin my day giving it to Yahweh and still end up cursing before the day's end? Abba, how could You let me fall? Mid-prayer, I answered myself, "Because I am doomed to hell already." As I spoke those words, the Lord spoke to me as a Father speaks to His daughter, and He said, "If you want to know who you are daughter, study the women before you." At that moment, I knew He answered me, and that morning at 0300 hrs., I began chronicling my journey through the Women of the Bible, starting with Eve.

In 2022, the Lord tugged on me to read the Book of Proverbs and that 31 days of Proverbs was in a little room called *Conversations of Life* where we visualized as I would open with, "Ya'll we're at the coffee house, and we've pulled the table together; grab your favorite beverage and let's glean the scriptures." This became a safe space to share my love of the Bible with women worldwide. On the 31st day, no one wanted the room to end, but me. "Lord," I said, "everyone wants to study the Book of Psalm, but Lord," I said, "that's 150 days, and that will be my entire Summer." I thought to myself all the things I am not: I am not a theologian, I am not a pastor, and I am certainly not a teacher.

Think of a time you've been tasked to do something. Does it typically begin with fear, followed by confirmations to support that fear? My first thought, "I'll pray about it." Typically, the I am thoughts cause my prayers to begin with, "Lord, I know You're not asking me to do this, it's the enemy setting me up to fail." The following day, I was in a state of prayer because my spirit was warring with my flesh. As I prepared for sleep, I prayed to the Lord and He spoke so clearly to me, *"No one, having put his hand to the plow, and looking back, is fit for the kingdom of God,"* a familiar scripture, Luke 9:62.

The Lord speaks to me through Scripture, so I knew He was calling me to continue. I said, "I am willing to do whatever You would have me to do but Lord, I am not enough." I was reasoning with God. I went to bed and dreamed a dream so vivid there was no disputing it came from the Lord. There was a beautiful table set but no ends on the table. The table was beautiful, and everyone was waiting for me to join. The Lord was there. A silhouette was how He looked; no color at all, just a visible outline, not ghostly. He had hands that I could feel. He had His right hand on my back and the other arm ushering me to what appeared to be the center of the table. Everyone was excited to have me join, and I was saying, "Lord, I need to get my cake. Everyone loves my pound cake. I have to go and get my pound cake," and He said gently, "Sit and eat, everything you need is already at the table." He began ushering me with His left arm to sit, while gently guiding me with the right hand, on my back, closer to the table, while everyone seated was celebrating my arrival.

As I write out this dream, I realize it was not a feast for the room I was about to host, but a feast for the many who accepted the assignment. It was like the picture of the Lord's supper, but He gave me His seat. I woke up and knew I was going to do the study of the Book of Psalm. Not because I grew an overwhelming sense of confidence, but the doubt that plagued my ability was replaced with trust in a sweet Savior that gave me His seat to feast at a table just like He bore the Cross for my countless sins. This project was also that assignment and making the choice to read this book and study the Women of the Bible is your assignment.

This anthology is like the Lord's table I dreamed. It's a gathering of a group of ladies who met on an app and decided to feast at the Lord's table. As we feasted on His Word, the Lord charged me with offering the opportunity to partner in this anthology.

This book is about modernizing the Women in the Bible, so you will see these ladies beyond the pages of the sacred text, but you see her, and in seeing her, you see yourself, "I am Her."

As you begin to read about the Women of the Bible, I will ask of you, as I asked of the ladies who joined me in writing this anthology, who, what, where, when, and why? Who is this woman? What did she do? Where is the Lord taking you as you read? When does her story intersect with your own life? Why is she written in the scripture? How is God speaking to you through her life? Please look beyond the written story and look for relevance today. As I share about Eve, I want to ask the Lord what "fruit" has tempted me. For Eve, it was fruit. For me, it appears as gluttony, idolatry, unforgiveness, and fear. Just like Eve, it separates us all from Christ. I pray that you will see Her. Chronicle your journey. Replace those chains with God's pearls of Wisdom. The Word of the Lord says,

"And suddenly there was a great earthquake, so that the foundations of the prison were shaken; and immediately all the doors were opened and everyone's bands were loosed" (Acts 16:20, AMP).

The Word says, *"the kingdom of heaven is like unto a merchant man, seeking goodly pearls: who, when he had found one pearl of great price, went and sold all that he had, and bought it"* (Matthew 13:45, KJV).

The Lord wants to free us, *"Shake off your dust; rise up, sit enthroned, Jerusalem. Free yourself from the chains on your neck, Daughter Zion, now a captive"* (Isaiah 52:2, NIV).

Chapter One

I am Her... Eve

Nycholle Woolfolk-Gater

I am her; she is me. Eve is known as the mother of all living; she is our beginning.

A Limited Mindset

When I pondered Heaven, as a young adult, it seemed impossible that a God who created this beautiful place ever had me, Nycholle Jamel Woolfolk, in that vision. Shame, the cost of my sin, marred the view of myself and how my Heavenly Father saw me. I closely related to the stiff neck individuals that disgusted God. An unwed mother, full-time caregiver, fatherless daughter, and "you asked for it" survivor were labels that I saw reflected back to me in the mirror and in the eyes of the women in my community and in the Church. These labels given to me by society were the ones accepted I wore shamefully like the *Scarlet Letter* I was required to read in Literature class, they were pinned on me.

As a young woman growing up in the Church, I saw myself through so many scriptures in the Bible but I never had the biblical understanding or knowledge to see myself the way God saw me. In Sunday school classes, I would hear about the wonderful God that loved me and gave His life for me and then in adult service, I would hear the Pastor in the pulpit tell a different story; oftentimes, minus the love. The young adult and later wife, I saw myself as shameful Eve who ate the fruit, or Vashti who did not come when her husband called, and Bathsheba whose bathing enticed King David. Pastors have preached from the pulpits the stories of these women and many others out of biblical imbalance. I have lived in shame, as a believer, because the women who looked like me and sounded like me were shamed from the pulpit. This book is in no way an attempt to bash or degrade men or pastors, but to encourage and uplift women and possibly enlighten the men who love them to see through our Heavenly Father's lens of our creation.

Enlightened by My Heavenly Father

In 2005, the Lord led me to study the Women of the Bible after praying, "Lord, why is it that I do the very thing I don't want to do?" He revealed the answers through stories of the incredible women before me. The more I studied, the more I prayed and cried. I begged for forgiveness because I was not living in accordance with how I was created. I realized every woman needs to know who they are according to God's Word. In June of 2022, the Lord guided me to gather a group of women alongside me to write this anthology. I was envisioning twenty-one to forty women; however, I believe all along the Lord showed me the total number would be less. He continued to say Jesus had twelve disciples. I am in no way comparing myself to Jesus, but I was thinking He was telling me not to be so exclusive in the selection because He was going to do a work in them through this project. Well, that is true. He has done a work through all of us; I believe He has chosen me to serve as a mother, if you will, in birthing something beautiful out of this assignment. So today, I share Eve, as I feel I am truly qualified, by my Father, to write her story to His daughters.

The Making of a Woman

The mother of all living! Eve is the only woman we will discuss that was named by her husband, Adam. He called her "woman". *"This is now bone of my bones, and flesh of my flesh: She shall be called Woman, because she was taken out of Man"* (Genesis 2:23, KJV). Eve lived in God's Garden, the Garden of Eden. There was no want in the Garden: she lived free of conflict, distraction, and chaos.

We will look at Eve in two parts before and after the fruit.

*"The Lord **formed** man from the dust of the ground, and breathed into his nostrils the breath of life; and man became a living soul"* (Genesis 2:7, KJV).

Man was **formed** and then given an **assignment**, *"And the Lord took the man, put him into the garden of Eden to dress it and to keep it"* (Genesis 2:15, KJV). God formed man and immediately gave the assignment to dress, which in Hebrew means abad to work, serve, and till the land. Keep in Hebrew means *shamar* and it means to hedge about, to guard the garden. Keep in mind, God had just rested and blessed all of His work before He even created Man. However, in God's own observation, He recognized, *"it is not good that the man should be alone; I will make him an help meet for him"* (Genesis 2:18, KJV).

This is an interesting word scholars translated here, "a help meet." So, *help*, when used as a noun, is to assist someone. *Meet* is a verb which relays the meaning, to come into the presence of someone. It is clear that "help meet" was intended to be translated to help meet someone's needs. In other translations, it reads, *a helper comparable to him* (NKJV), and again in another version it reads, *helper meet [suitable, adapted, complementary]* (Amplified). I want to note something here, every time someone attempts to translate the meaning of an original text, the meaning is diluted from the original intent. I would like to think that it has been unintentional, but how often do you hear people say help mate vs help meet?

"And the Lord God caused a deep sleep to fall upon Adam, and he slept: and he took one of his ribs, and closed up the flesh instead thereof; and the rib, which the Lord God had taken from the man, made he a woman, and brought her unto the man" (Genesis 2:21-22, KJV).

Please notice the language difference here, the Lord **formed** man, which is *yatsar* in Hebrew, meaning to mold into a form as a potter. This is the same word used to describe that *out of the ground the Lord God formed every beast of the field…* (Genesis 2:19a, KJV). However, the Lord **made** woman, in Hebrew it means *banah* to build, obtain, make and repair. The Lord used something He already **formed** to **make** woman. God refers to woman as her role, *I will make him an help meet for him.*

Help meet, what an interesting expression used to introduce the assignment of the Woman. Just like Man, Woman has an assignment, and purpose. "Help," as written in the KJV, is recorded twenty-one times in Scripture and is simply translated in the Concordance Bible as `*ezer*, meaning to help. However, the word "meet," scholars chose not to translate. Help meet is only written twice in Genesis and thereby diminishing the `ezer to simply mean the mediocre task of helping. In the scriptures that reference `ezer were cries for help in times of serious trouble. Remember, God's original assignment for man was to dress and keep the Garden. Several scholars over the years have actually stated `ezer with the word translated meet is actually translated in Hebrew as kenegdô. Although they are very difficult to translate, it is agreed to be understood as a helper and counterpart alongside him.

God gave the woman an assignment, a task of her own. Is it so hard to believe that God made woman a partner alongside someone with purpose? Consider women in the Bible like Deborah, Esther, Jael, Sarah, Mary, Abigail, Elizabeth, Hagar, Tamar, and the hundreds of women whose stories have yet to be told. It is only fitting that women have a purpose and assignment dependent and independent of men. This writing, my intention, is to broaden the viewpoint of women and men who are willing to abandon the limiting beliefs that hold women hostage to silence the giants that reside within.

God's Word, My Vantage Point
To think that our Father observed man, looked at his qualities, and said, "It's not good for man to be alone; I will make him an help meet for him," demonstrates God's intention in Woman. In general terms, God is saying, "What does the world I created need, that man does not already possess?" I believe, God knew He needed to make a complement to Man that would be opposite in anatomy, as women have eggs and are able to birth life, protect his heart, support his goals, and provide a safe landing space for Man.

Why did God choose the rib? Woman was made using a rib from Man, not dust. He's God, He created the heavens and the Earth and yet when He created Woman, He caused a deep sleep to fall over Adam and removed one of his ribs (Genesis 2:21).

The rib is a long curved bone; we have twenty-four ribs attached forming a rib cage. The rib cage has three functions: to protect, to support, and respiration (breath). I can get in-depth with the study of the rib cage; however, I wanted you to understand as women, we were not haphazardly created, but purposefully made. We are crafted from the most vital part of the male body, the rib cage, which encloses and protects the heart and lungs. Let's ponder the breath. You remember the original breath God breathed into the nostrils when He created man, the rib cage that protects that breath was used to make Woman. We were created from the rib cage that supported the original Breath of God.

Wow! We are Woman, hear us roar!!! I believe our role, in the beginning, and also today, is summed up in the function of the rib. The rib cage supports, or provides, the framework for the chest, abdomen, and back. The rib cage is flexible and expands and contracts for respiration.

"The rib which the Lord God had taken from the man He made (fashioned, formed) into a woman and He brought her and presented her to the man" (Genesis 2:22, AMP).

Man was placed in the Garden, prior to Woman, and tasked to dress and keep it. Woman was made and given to Man. We are a gift! Now, the scripture says, in every translation… *"and brought her to the man"* (Genesis 2:22). When God made Woman, our intended and current purpose is to be a gift, not for the temporary pleasure of satisfying flesh but for the life goal of pursuing a greater, purposeful calling to build and to protect.

Wisdom through the Lens of Fruit

Woman was not called *Eve* until after she ate the fruit. Woman was innocent and free to roam about the Garden and explore. She is naked, which shows that she was free of inhibitions, or restrictions, not being exposed to anything but the beauty and splendor of God's design. I don't believe we are able to fathom the true sense of nakedness before God. We can't compare nakedness in the Garden of Eden to the nakedness of a nudist camp, or when you remove clothing after a long day at work. There's a freedom that you feel when you have something that you are loosed from; in this case, clothing.

My finite mind can only fathom this picture as that of a babe learning to run or crawl away from the restraints of a diaper, or onesie. No, the true nakedness that Eve felt our finite minds can't fathom the full extent of what it means to be before the Living God free and pure. Woman walks around in exploration and awe of God's Creation. She is birthed into a wonderful existence and she is insatiable to see and learn everything her mind can hold. She did not have the foretold stories of a mother or grandmother to help her rationalize her decisions. She saw her husband talk with the Lord God in the Garden and so she ventured out on her own to explore her place in this awestruck glory she was learning to call home.

I see Eve, *I am Her*! She walks unsuspecting of what's lurking. Like Eve, I remember the times I trusted people with my heart and they abused me. I took their word at face value and paid dearly for my ignorance. Yes, *I am Her*! Unbeknownst to Eve, the serpent was lurking about waiting. The serpent saw Woman and could smell the hunger for knowledge, probably before he even saw her. When the Woman was created, the scripture verse following Adam calling her "woman" states... *"man shall leave his father and mother and be joined to his wife, and they shall become one flesh"* (Genesis 2:24, NKJV).

The Lord clearly said, *"Of every tree of the garden you may freely eat; but of the tree of the knowledge of good and evil you shall not eat, for in the day that you eat of it you shall surely die"* (Genesis 2:16-17 NKJV). When the serpent questioned Eve for clarity, it was deception at its best.

"Has God indeed said, 'You shall not eat of every tree of the garden'?" and Woman answers, *"We may eat the fruit of the trees of the garden; but of the fruit of the tree which is in the midst of the garden, God has said, 'You shall not eat it, nor shall you touch it, lest you die'"* (Genesis3:1-3, NKJV)

The Woman understood what God told her. She was clear. Satan, with subtilty, stroked her desire for wisdom and knowledge causing her to eat the fruit and subsequently, give the fruit to Adam. Paul uses this example to share with the Corinthians how subtle sin leads us astray as he shares, *"But I fear, lest somehow, as the serpent deceived Eve by his craftiness, so your minds may be corrupted from the simplicity that is in Christ"* (2 Corinthian 11:3, NKJV).

I am reminded of David as he shares, *"Behold, I was shapen in iniquity; and in sin did my mother conceive me"* (Psalm 51:5, KJV).

In the Garden of Eden, Woman was like a newborn babe. She utilized her senses to explore her new surroundings; the sense of taste, the sense of smell, and the sense of touch. As I ponder and pray, I ask, "Lord, why do I desire the very thing we don't need?" Woman had everything she could desire right before her eyes yet she still wanted the very thing she was not to eat. Not much has changed today. Women like to test the water, to make sure it's hot. I certainly do, I pride myself on the fact that I am not a follower, so I seek new territories and I believe it is my natural instinct to do the very thing someone tells me I cannot. Telling me I can't do something makes me want it that much more. We have slogans like, "If you want it bad enough, go get it."

This very desire and drive that is in us was in Woman. She desired to see those things she had not seen, and taste those things she had not tasted. The serpent knew this. He was waiting for the moment. I believe he could smell desire all over her, so he simply enticed what was already inside of her. The verse that precedes the serpent is worthy of noting here.

"And Adam said, this is now bone of my bones, and flesh of my flesh: she shall be called Woman because she was taken out of Man. Therefore shall a man leave his father and his mother, and shall cleave unto his wife: and they shall be one flesh" (Genesis 2:23-24, KJV).

So, as Woman begins exploring and meets the serpent and is enticed, she is able to entice Man. Man understood, he was the recipient of a good gift. He began to cleave to Eve, so when she offered fruit, he did partake.

"So when the woman saw that the tree was good for food, that it was pleasant to the eyes, and a tree desirable to make one wise, she took its fruit and ate. She also gave to her husband with her and he ate" (Genesis 3:6, NKJV).

Cleave is *dabaq* in Hebrew and properly means to impinge, cling, and adhere. It's understandable that Man ate the fruit.

For a moment, I would like to ponder on the "knowledge" Woman was seeking. I tried to understand *da'ath*, the Hebrew word translated into knowledge. I attempted to rely on my own ability to research and study. After allotting hours of study, I realized I had to go to the source, my Creator. As I studied, *da'ath* and *yada`*, the Hebrew word for knowing, I went deeper and studied word origins and I began to see this was less about this Anthology and more about my desire to have greater *da'ath* or *yada`*. I prayed and asked, "God, is this relevant to this assignment or am I charting my own course?"

My answer came from the life of Eve. I was seeking knowledge. It was the subtilty of what I was seeking. That knowledge opened my eye and ear gate to good and evil. I am grateful for the awareness of my Heavenly Father. I believe knowledge is a fluid word and in today's culture, we all seek knowledge to better ourselves and to grow. However, it's the heart posture you have for anything you pursue that determines the fruit you plant. Eve's heart posture was towards being like God,

"And the serpent said unto the woman, Ye shall not surely die: For God doth know that in the day ye eat thereof, then your eyes shall be

opened, and ye shall be as gods, knowing good and evil" (Genesis 3:4-5 KJV).

Eve's posture was to be like God. I am reminded as David continues in the Book of Psalm, *"Behold, thou desirest truth in the inward parts: And in the hidden part thou shalt make me to know wisdom"* (Psalm 51:6, KJV).

Fruit Sewn is Grown and Reaped

I have often heard the debate, it's all Eve's fault; that's why women are the weaker link. I am not here to debate fault, it is clear the serpent approached Eve. The question I have pondered is why did the serpent approach Eve and not Adam? If the goal of Satan is to tear down the Kingdom of God, why do so via a woman? Scripture tells us,

"Or else how can one enter into a strong man's house, and spoil his goods, except he first bind the strong man? and then he will spoil his house" (Matthew 12:29, KJV).

I am not sure if I will ever know why but in prayer and in time with the Holy Spirit, I have grown to understand that there is something in me that makes me a target. The fact that I am able to give birth to something, or someone, makes me a target. Eve was enticed with fruit. Let's ponder that for a moment, she was in God's Garden, so there was no need for anything. She was not hungry. She didn't desire the fruit for nutrition; it was food the serpent used to entice a desire to open her eyes to wisdom. The scripture says,

"So when the woman saw that the tree was good for food, that it was pleasant to the eyes, and a tree desirable to make one wise, she took its

fruit and ate. She also gave to her husband with her, and he ate" (Genesis 3:6, NKJV).

So the question to myself is, "What is the enemy enticing you with Nycholle?" I will ask you, "What is the enemy, the serpent, using to entice you?" He enticed Eve with fruit to open her up to wisdom; I have been enticed by the spoken flattery words of men who meant me no good, and the stylish new clothes that made me look like a million bucks only to put me in debt. I didn't need the clothing and I was not going any place that warranted or required that I looked like a million bucks, so why go into debt? I did not need the flattery of men because my natural father and mother always told me I was beautiful, so I didn't need anyone to tell me what had always been spoken over me.

Like Eve, I was in search of those things my flesh desired and it didn't require a reason. Scripture tells us, *"Walk in the Spirit, and ye shall not fulfill the lust of the flesh. For the flesh lustest against the Spirit, and the Spirit against the flesh: and these are contrary the one to the other: so that ye cannot do the things that ye would. But if ye be led of the Spirit ye are not under the law. Now the works of the flesh are manifest, which are these; Adultery, fornication, uncleanness, lasciviousness, idolatry, witchcraft, hatred, variance, emulations, wrath, strife, seditions, heresies, envyings, murders, drunkenness, revellings, and such like: of the which I tell you before as I have also told you in time past, that they which do such things shall not inherit the kingdom of God. But the fruit of the Spirit is love, joy, peace, longsuffering, gentleness, goodness, faith, meekness, temperance: against such there is no law"* (Galatians 5:16-23, KJV).

This passage of scripture was my breakthrough passage! My epiphany was realized when I began to see that I was sowing seeds of flesh and expected to reap the harvest of the Fruit of the Spirit. It took me years to see the correlation between the "fruit" Eve ate, as it was written fruit in the Bible and not an apple, and the fruit written all throughout Scripture. Our ministry is all about sewing, harvesting, and reaping. Everything we do, or say, is a seed that brings forth life and we reap that which we have sewn. I have the ability to use my words to lift up or tear down. I can walk in the room and be the thermostat or the thermometer by bringing a calm to the storm, or being the storm. I have been both. I have the ability to lift my husband or tear him down with my words, and I have done both. Our words hurt! It is important to be impeccable with our words to use them to encourage and heal.

Eve is known as the woman/mother who introduced us all to sin. She was deceived by the serpent and ate of the fruit of the forbidden tree. *Eve* and Adam were driven out of Eden. The Bible doesn't share a journal of the day-to-day struggles of the new life of Adam and Eve. The Bible doesn't share their pillow talks at night. We don't get to see if they argued over whose fault it was that they were driven out of Eden. This is interesting because men and women have argued that point for years. I can relate to the mental torment I carry myself through when I know the enemy has used me. We carry the burdens of our spouses. Looking after Adam day after day, she saw his body bruised with callouses from hard days of work; I am certain that was a present reminder of her sin.

After leaving the Garden of Eden, Eve was able to conceive children. The ability to conceive was a blessing in her eyes as Eve says, *"I have acquired a man from the Lord"* (Genesis 4:1, KJV). Eve gave birth to two sons Cain, a tiller of the ground and Abel, keeper of the sheep.

Before we can even celebrate the birth, we see sin cast its ugly head. Cain, out of jealousy, killed Abel. In addition to carrying the burden of being banished from the Garden of Eden, she was now the mother of the first murderer and the first mother to have to bury a son.

I can't begin to rationalize the despair Eve was feeling at the loss of her son. I have wondered over the years why my pastors did not talk about her beyond eating the fruit. She most likely blamed herself for introducing sin. I often wonder if she blamed her parenting skills for the jealousy between her sons. Had she not already experienced her punishment? *"Unto the woman he said, I will greatly multiply thy sorrow and thy conception; in sorrow thou shalt bring forth children; and thy desire shall be to thy husband, and he shall rule over thee"* (Genesis 3:16, KJV). Her punishment was continual from generation to generation. This was her life outside of Eden and I believe the revelation of this hit Eve when she lost her son, Abel.

Many would have curled up and lost hope. After all, she introduced sin and lost her son at the hands of her eldest. Here is where we must be reminded that no matter how far we stray away from ABBA, He is always right there with us. In my darkest hours, He has never left me nor forsaken me. I think of Eve, as *I am her* and ponder my own life. I am still living my story out. I am a lot wiser today than I was a year ago. I have learned to trust God no matter what my situation feels like or looks like. I often tell people, "Trace the Hand of God;" do so as if you are watering seeds. What I know for sure is when I spend more time tracing His hand, I take less time focusing on the problem. I have learned that everything in life teaches me something I will need in my forward. So, I ask you, take your eyes off whatever life is throwing you and trace His hand over it, water it with His Word! Eve's story didn't end with a banished son or a grave site to visit. Eve bore another son and named him Seth, *"for God has appointed another seed for me instead of Abel whom Cain killed." And as for Seth, to him also a son was born; and he named him Enos. Then men began to call on the name of the Lord"* (Genesis 4:26, NKJV).

I chose to write about Eve because I was on a journey of self-discovery and Eve was the first woman, the First Family, if you will. I asked the Lord, why do I do the things I don't want to do so easily? Why do I continue to self-sabotage? Why do I continue to sit in Church every Sunday and still use foul language? The Lord led me on a journey to study the Women of the Bible to see just where I came from. You see, if you don't know who you are, you will allow life and others to define you. You will attempt to define yourself but there's something about knowing that you know that the God who made the Heaven and Earth really did have you and me in mind. He really did have a plan for us when He made us.

My prayer for you as you read Eve is that you will be able to see yourself in her, just as I was able to see myself every woman I studied. I began to see just how much God loves me in the way He meticulously made me. I saw El Ohim and that allowed me fall in love with Him. I saw Him as ABBA Father, my Daddy! So, Eve opened the door for me to repent for the way I was living my life. Eve is this wonderful woman who the Lord has allowed me to not only hear, but *see* her. I see her in a hut watching from a far as her husband toils and labor. I see her watching the bitterness take root between her sons and feeling powerless to address it. I see her as she buries her son and then watches as another is banished. I see her sadness as she ponders her role. I ponder because *I am her*. As a mother of four children, I often say I am never happier than my saddest child. Mothers tend to feel the sadness of their children, their first heartache; how does Eve recover and find joy after losing two sons? As I walked out, I always prayed my children would never suffer from my past sins. Looking at Eve, I wonder if she blamed her sins for those of her sons. I became so familiar with Eve on this journey that I see her watching her sons at the doorway, and I hear the absence of sound in the home once occupied by children that are gone.

Blessings in the Lessons

My self-study of Eve has brought me so much joy. If we only look at the story of Eve from the lens of the fruit, we will miss the greater lesson to be learned from her life. Maybe for Eve it was the fruit, but what is the shame and sin you opened yourself up to? What is it that you need to leave at the altar of forgiveness? Adam and Eve's sin causes them to hide in shame and clothe themselves. When I found my true identity in my Heavenly Father's plan and purpose for my life through the story of the Women of the Bible, I could remove the clothing that I hid behind. I could remove the mask. There is a level of freedom that comes only from knowing who you are, a freedom that allows you to walk unapologetically in your purpose, like the women before you.

What we learn from Eve:
- You, woman of God, are created with a purpose.
- You, woman of God, are a gift from God.
- Satan is intimately attracted to your purpose and he will use all the tools in his arsenal to keep you from fulfilling your purpose.
- Sin separates us from God.
- Sin manifests itself in shame and guilt.
- Trace the Hand of God and not your problems.
- Fruit of the Spirit is the evidence of the Spirit of God.

I believe Eve is one of the least discussed women of the Bible and yet one the most relevant to the life of a woman. We learn so much from Eve. We learn about the penalty for her sins, but we also learn the "oneness" of a marriage. Despite the shame and guilt Eve undoubtedly experienced, she persevered. She found hope in being a helpmeet to Adam and mother to her children. We leave Eve, not the naive woman who was birthed in the Garden of Eden, a little tattered and worn by the scars of life. Death crossed her threshold and she buried a child, her child, and the other banished. She thought her womb was closed by the disgrace and shame of murder and death in the first family. God appointed her another seed, Seth, and he bore Enos, Scripture tells us, and men began to call on the name of the Lord.

Eve's story ends with a blessing and because of this blessing, I am reminded that joy does come in the morning. I encourage you to re-read the story of Eve through your lens, the Word tells us to, *"Study to shew thyself approved unto God, a workman that needeth not to be ashamed, rightly dividing the word of truth"* (2 Timothy 2:15, KJV). As you study, pause and pray for understanding. I am sharing Eve from the lens of a wife, mother, and grandmother; however, my earlier study of Eve was very different eighteen years ago. I had school-age children and was not a grandmother. I hadn't experienced the loss my mother or mother-in-love. Life has taught me a different lesson as I study Eve today and I pray you will search the scriptures and allow God's Word to transform your life.

Connect with Nycholle Woolfolk-Gater:
Website: www.nycholle.com
Email: info@nycholle.com
Phone: 571-699-5822

For products and resources, click on the QR Code below:

Ponder *I am Her*... Strings of Wisdom for reflection:

_____

_____

_____

_____

_____

_____

_____

_____

_____

_____

_____

_____

_____

_____

_____

_____

_____

_____

_____

_____

_____

_____

_____

_____

_____

_____

_____

_____

Chapter Two

I am Her... Lot's Wife

Nisaa Robinson

And yet, She Still Speaks

Y ou heard the call. The assignment is clear. And, if not the assignment, the direction, the focus, the attitude. You recognize what it will take to shift from where you are, to where you desire to be. You have been pleading with God to make a way for what you believe is next. You know there is greatness in you to be gifted to the world. Yet, you feel a tug ever so slightly or a forceful pull on your time, energy, and attention, causing you to look back at what was. Although, it is not quite what you want, or what you believe in your heart is purposed for you, it's not so bad, plus it's familiar and you know just how to move in that space.

Maybe you missed it. It wouldn't be the first time you missed the mark on understanding the leading of God. Maybe you misunderstood the instructions, and you are supposed to stay right where you are or return to a former, known way. I, like you, have experienced shifting back and forth about decisions, feeling concerned about what is ahead, and wondering, is it okay to just stay where I am. I mean, other people seem to be doing just fine in similar circumstances. I suppose thoughts of a similar nature ran through the mind of Lot's wife as she contemplated a whole new existence in response to an abrupt shift in her world.

Like so many of the experiences of my life, I didn't choose this focus on Lot's wife, rather it chose me. Have you ever found yourself deliberately in a space of saying yes to the things that bring discomfort, fear, resistance? See, that's where I was when the opportunity to walk alongside Lot's wife in this work was presented to me. And, while I wasn't sure of the meaning and didn't immediately identify the connections, I trusted it was purposeful, and just said, "Yes!" And I am grateful for the *yes*.

Lot's wife, as mentioned in the Bible, is an unnamed woman, a wife and mother, who some think to have been a native to Sodom, the land that was described as a land where the people did detestable things before God, and were haughty, apathetic, complacent, arrogant, overfed, and unconcerned; they did not help the poor and needy (Ezekiel 16:49-50; Jude 1:7). There is very little written of her in the scriptures, yet what is written is profound and necessary.

Before we get in too deep, let me start by sharing a little about myself. I have been married for over twenty years, to my high school sweetheart. For many of our early years together, I experienced others referring to me only in reference to him, without the use of my name.

Now listen, I was my own whole person with a growing sense of self and independence prior to entering a relationship with James. For whatever reason, I became known as *Byrd's girl*, then *James' wife*. Not Nisaa, no, Byrd's girl, then James' wife. I suppose it would be helpful to share that my husband, James, is also known as "Byrd" (like Bird). I don't know when or why it started, but many people in the neighborhood and connected peer groups referred to me this way. I mean in person, face to face as they were talking to me, not just as they referenced me in a story they were telling. So, needless to say, Lot's wife and I have this thing in common.

Now that I think about it, this also happened in reference to one of my brothers and one of my sisters. In certain circles, I was known as *Nixon's sister* and *Banisha's sister*, as well. Again, to my face, this is how people referred to me. I suppose there remain additional lessons to glean from that experience. It does allow me to connect to Lot's wife in this way. One lesson here is that "I am because I am," and being identified in connection with others is quite alright, and in no way diminishes my value. And, even if my name isn't mentioned, the impact of my existence is real and the same is true of Lot's wife. Real, and necessary.

While we are not certain of the beliefs of Lot's wife, we are told she was married to Lot, who was identified as a righteous man. I will make no assumptions regarding her beliefs or heart toward God. Additionally, let's establish there will be no bashing of Lot's wife. We will look to glean what we can from what we know of her story.

The Familiar
Lot's wife is known for disobeying the instructions of an angel, looking back toward Sodom and Gomorrah, and turning into a pillar of salt (being destroyed).

"But his wife looked back from behind him, and she became a pillar of salt" (Genesis 19:26, KJV).

The logical question is why did she look back? Did she look back in sadness for others, perhaps family, or friends who were not rescued? Did she look back angry that the land she was familiar with and desired to dwell was being destroyed? Did she look back to simply get a view of the destruction occurring? Did she look back in fear that her needs wouldn't be met along the way or in the new destination?

Backstory

Lot's wife is first mentioned in the 19th Chapter of Genesis and again in the 17th Chapter of Luke.

This chapter is indeed focused on Lot's wife. Given there isn't much shared about Lot's wife, we will review what we know about Lot and scriptures leading to the key scripture focused on Lot's wife, so that we have a level of context and understanding.

Lot was the grandson of Terah, son of Haran, and nephew of Abram (Abraham, identified as the father of faith and the Jewish people). He was likely born in Ur of the Chaldeans. Terah and Lot traveled with Abraham, and when Abraham responded to the call to journey to the Promised Land.

Along their journey, while in Canaan, Abraham and Lot's servants were in strife over grazing areas for their herds of livestock. In response to this, Abraham and Lot agreed to separate and settle in different areas with Abraham giving Lot first choice of land. Lot chose the land of the plain of Jordan, near Sodom and Gomorrah, because of the rich pastureland (Genesis 13:10-11). Lot's choice, appearing influenced by a "greener grass" attitude was not advantageous, as the wickedness of Sodom was very great. Well, to be fair, in this case, the grass was "greener" near Sodom, but greener did not prove to be better; quite the contrary.

We pick up the story with Lot and his family living in the land of Sodom, where all manner of wickedness occurred. We are not told specifically that Lot's wife was a native of the land. However, it would be logical to deduce this as plausible. Either way, their family remained dwelling in a land where the wickedness was great.

The Bible tells us Lot was a righteous man (2 Peter 2:7-8). While that may be so, we all know that the environment and culture in which one lives can be quite influential on the beliefs, and attitudes developed by those in the environment, which drive thoughts and behaviors. Avoiding influence and sustaining righteous living is challenging in most environments, let alone in a land where the sin was significant enough that the outcry against its people was great enough to warrant God's wrath.

In the 19th chapter of Genesis, we learn of the gravity of the great sin in Sodom and Gomorrah. Two angels sent by God delivered the message that the cry of the land had waxen greatly before the Lord, and they were sent to destroy the land. We see God's grace demonstrated in that the angels were sent to rescue Lot and his family to prevent them from being destroyed. The angels warned Lot that if they did not obey and flee the land, Lot and his family would be consumed in the iniquity of the land.

"And when the morning arose, then the angels hastened Lot, saying, Arise, take thy wife, and thy two daughters, which are here; lest thou be consumed in the iniquity of the city. And while he lingered, the men laid hold upon his hand, and upon the hand of his wife, and upon the hand of his two daughters; the Lord being merciful unto him: and they brought him forth and set him without the city. And it came to pass, when they had brought them forth abroad, that he said, Escape for thy life; look not behind thee, neither stay thou in all the plain; escape to the mountain, lest thou be consumed" (Genesis 19:15-17, KJV).

Verses 15-17 of Chapter 19 tell of the specific instructions given to Lot and his family to leave the land. We also see that there was a lack of responsiveness, or sense of urgency, among Lot and his family to respond to the instructions. Lot is then told to take those of his house who were present and leave the land. It would be multiple urgings from the angels before there was a response by Lot and his family. In fact, the angels physically led Lot and his wife by the hand, because Lot lingered despite previous warnings.

It sparks curiosity here that they had to be led in this way. Further, Lot's wife was led toward safety by the angels and not her husband. Was this typical? Was Lot one to lack leadership in his marriage and household? Perhaps, the dynamics between Lot and his wife were such that each developed a nonchalant attitude toward their relationship, and life? Was this a display of a significant level of desensitization regarding care and concern one typically has for their own life?

This causes me to recall the reality of living in a neighborhood where sirens, fights, and gunshots are so frequent that you are not phased, you no longer duck down as an effort toward safety. And, when you hear of the latest tragedy or suspected planned dangerous activity, you are not moved emotionally or physically. How many can relate to the experiences just described? There are many with similar experiences who longed for the opportunity to be free from the trauma of it all; yet had difficulty moving on, even when the escape route and instructions were set before them. Be mindful to note the specificity of instructions given in verse 17, as it is key in our exploration of Lot's wife and what she may teach us.

The Familiar Dilemma

Before we get beside ourselves and venture off into the deep and spiritual, I offer you (us, really) a reality moment. I venture to say that most individuals can recall times in your life when you thought back, reconsidered, or longed for a past relationship, friendship, life situation, or circumstance that you knew was no good for you, to you or anyone else for that matter, or perhaps you even returned to said situation. Oh, maybe that part was just for me... just in case there is one other reader who can relate, let me say... I have worked with hundreds of women, and it is a common story that despite red flags, unhealthy dynamics, and detrimental patterns, they returned to a relationship that didn't serve them, to use an example.

It is common to hear stories of women recognizing family and so-called friends are taking advantage of them, and yet they return to the unhealthy and harmful (for both parties) relationship. In both scenarios, sometimes individuals can see the impending doom of the circumstances, yet they continue to think of what was, or the possibility of changing the situation rather than turning away and never looking back.

So, let's not view ourselves as too far removed from Lot's wife's dilemma and circumstance that we miss the many lessons she gives us. You see, your next is now. The decision that you face right there, at that crossroad. You cannot receive what is next while holding on to what is now. And, sweetie, you want to let it go anyway. You just don't know what is next, and that is scary. You have been praying for a breakthrough, a refuge, an escape hatch. I get it. Been there. There right now in some areas. Just understand, the solution may not always appear immediately desirable. And this, my love, is why we live by faith. And, if we knew the whole story, or could see the entire path, the journey wouldn't require faith.

I am reminded by Lot's wife's story, that while some of my human reasoning may seem rational, and logical, there is never a good or acceptable reason to disobey what the Lord has said or instructed. To do so communicates a few issues.

1. Lack of trust in God.
2. Pride in believing I can think on a level equal with God to decide against what has been said/revealed.
3. Lack of faith in God as a provider.

Of course, these aren't usually surface or conscious level thoughts, but the deeper, subconscious level of belief showing up in my actions or inaction. This point brings emphasis to the importance of regular practices that encourage introspection and surrounding oneself with other mature believers who can support discipleship, growth, and development.

It is important to understand that there is always a bigger picture than what I can see or understand, and that God acts in my best interest, whether I can comprehend His instructions, or not.

God is Trustworthy

I don't know about you, but I know I have more than enough evidence that operating in a self-reliant manner doesn't end well, and that God is deserving of my trust and reliance.

"Likewise also as it was in the days of Lot; they did eat, they drank, they bought, they sold, they planted, they builded; But the same day that Lot went out of Sodom it rained fire and brimstone from heaven, and destroyed them all. Even thus shall it be in the day when the Son of man is revealed. In that day, he which shall be upon the housetop, and his stuff in the house, let him not come down to take it away: and he that is in the field, let him likewise not return back. Remember Lot's wife. Whosoever shall seek to save his life shall lose it; and whosoever shall lose his life shall preserve it" (Luke 17:28-33, KJV).

Let us learn, or be reminded, that God will preserve and protect us when we are in His will, and this requires trust that His instructions are beneficial. To think or behave contrary, without trust in His goodness toward me, leaves me feeling like it is necessary to save, protect, and preserve myself. This increases the potential for me to act from a self-reliant position, which can ultimately influence detrimental results, as we are reminded by Jesus in Luke 17:28-33.

Getting to the Heart: Definitions, Impact, and Meaning

If you are anything like me, you want to get understanding, and I appreciate getting clarity around the words chosen and the intended meaning in general conversation, let alone in the Bible. Let's return to the story of Lot's wife and review the definition of a few of the key words from the key scripture (Genesis 19:26) using the lexicon for the Hebrew language, which helps us gain greater insight, as the Hebrew language can have very rich meanings and depths of the use of the same word.

"But his wife looked back from behind him, and she became a pillar of salt" Genesis 19:26, KJV.

Looked back: nabat (naw-bat')
To scan, i.e. look intently at; by implication, to regard with pleasure, favor or care (cause to) behold, consider, look (down), regard, have respect, see.

Lot's wife lost her life because she "looked back." Based on study of the scripture and the meaning of the words used to explain her action, this was more than just a glance over the shoulder; it was a look of longing that indicated reluctance to leave, or a desire to return. Whatever the case, the point is she was called to desert everything to save her life, but she did not let go, and the cost was her life. In Judaism, Lot's wife became a symbol for a rebellious unbeliever.

The act of looking back is a demonstration and reflection of what occurs in the heart. It displays an attitude of disagreement, disapproval, or denial, even if in the act of partial obedience. The rebellion is to refuse to place full trust in God and His guidance. God is worthy of our full reliance and trust, the type of trust spoken of in Proverbs 3:5-6. Lot's wife's behavior demonstrates for us that partial obedience still carries risk of danger, and exposure to the ways of the world. Full trust in God is demonstrated through full obedience.

I don't know about you, but I know there are many stories I can tell of halfway doing the "right thing"... and things didn't work out. What was the issue? I didn't have full buy-in, belief, or investment of my behavior and paid the cost for the lack of full investment.

When "the Son of Man is revealed," it will be time for people to move/flee. There will be no time to take anything along, to look back or around. If you see the sign when you are on the roof (a rooftop deck with exterior stairs was a common feature of houses at the time), you should not even take time to go into the house to gather up your possessions (Luke 17:30-32). Lot's wife is an example of what will happen if you linger, or look back. If you try to save your life (that is, the things, people, experiences that your life is made of), you will lose everything. Leave it all to save your life.

This message is appropriate for living a righteous life dedicated to the Lord in this world. It may be necessary for you to flee the former thoughts, attitudes, assumptions, habits, relationships, and environments that are familiar, so God can place you where you can flourish in relationship with Him and impact your world and THE world. You cannot grab hold of what God has for you, or what is next for you, while you are holding what was/is, or what you think it is supposed to be. Do the work (spirit and soul work) necessary to become a willing, trusting vessel fit for the master's use, that you may save your life, and live life more abundantly.

Jesus also used the statement "whoever wants to save his life shall lose it" in a number of different contexts (Matthew 10:39; 16:25; Mark 8:35, Luke 9:24; 17:33). Regardless of the specifics of the context, following Jesus requires turning away from the offerings of this world. Attempting to "save/preserve/protect yourself" can be synonymous with "looking back." Attachment to our former life and the perceived securities can cause us to lose the opportunity for life as God designs for us and our very lives, and Lot's wife is the illustration and example that we would do well to remember that God is able to keep us, provide for us, and he can be trusted.

Lot's wife looked back. We don't know how long, but the word choice suggests more than a glance. She turned and witnessed fire and brimstone consuming everything she knew. Then, it consumed her. In Hebrew, this term for "looked back" means more than a quick look. It means "to regard, to consider, to pay attention to." We are not told in the scripture that her death was punishment for valuing her old life so much that she hesitated in obeying, or if it was the consequence of her reluctance to move quickly. Either she identified with and potentially longed for the city and/or she neglected to operate with full obedience to God's warning, and she was consumed.

And she became a pillar: ntsiyb (nets-eeb')
Something stationary, i.e. a prefect, a military post, a statue, garrison, officer, pillar.

The scripture does not state clearly whether Lot's wife was covered in the salt that rained down with the brimstone or if her remains were dusted with a coating of salt after the fact. She is described as a "pillar." In Hebrew, pillar refers to a garrison or a deputy, that is, something set to watch over something else. The image of Lot's wife standing watch over the Dead Sea area, where no life can exist is a poignant reminder to us not to look back or turn back from our profession of faith, and to follow Christ without hesitation. She, who is not given a name, stands and still speaks. We are listening.

Of salt: melach (meh'-lakh)
Powder, i.e. (specifically) salt (as easily pulverized and dissolved, salt (-pit).

Why Salt?
Salt is a widely used substance for various purposes. Salt is used to preserve, season, cleanse, and purify. They used it in many areas of life. It was used to season their food (Job 6:6). They also rubbed salt on their infants (Ezekiel 16:4), and utilized salt in their offerings and sacrifices (Leviticus 2:13).

Jesus calls believers the salt of the Earth in (Matthew 5:13, Mark 9:50, and Luke 14:34). Jesus calls us to remember Lot's wife. Whoever tries to keep his life will lose it, and whoever loses his life will preserve it" (Luke 17:32-33). This is a warning against false security. Lot's wife turned back possibly looking toward all she lost and all that created a sense of security. Despite the reality that all of it was being destroyed, perhaps she longed for that which she had known as her safety, security, and comfort. Her demise is a reminder to seek these things in relationship with God and follow the leading and instructions He gives for righteous living. For, if you seek the Kingdom and His righteousness, all these things shall be added unto you (Matthew 6:33, KJV).

A column of what appears to be salt and soil on the Jordanian side of the Dead Sea is believed to be the remains of Lot's Wife and is known as such. The visual of Lot's wife standing as a pillar of salt communicates and presents the opportunity to be preserved through application of the lessons learned from her life and how it ended.

Her story can season and preserve us, and prevent us from actions that put our salvation, future, and representation at risk.

Let's be real, we all have experiences of starting out, seemingly committed, then find ourselves back where we started from, or quite close. Or maybe that is just me.

Links with Lot's Wife
In addition, the point on being unnamed, our stories also parallel in that I can identify times in my life when I believed I was to go in a direction and rather than executing immediate and full obedience, I delayed, started out, and stopped in process, or wondered if the new path was the right direction or should I return to a former thing, or at least considered if I should go a different way. All demonstrations of a lack of full obedience to the instructions. I mean, which of us hasn't found ourselves at the decision point, or crossroads, if you will. The truth of the matter is, all day long, we stand at the decision line on various matters, not the least of which, will we live in faith and obedience, or in our own perceptions and strength?

Obviously, she trusted (or was compliant) enough to leave, follow a portion of the instructions and her husband, in that she accompanied Lot as the family left the land, eventually and just about, by force. However, as we see in the scripture, partial obedience does not suffice, and lingering beliefs and attitudes associated with our former life presents a significant risk for our future.

Remember my lack of understanding the relevant connection to the story of Lot's wife I mentioned previously? As I write this, I am seeking God for clarity around significant life decisions that will shift me into a place of the unknown and discomfort. Yet, I believe the shift is a part of the course of my life and will ultimately present a blessing for my family and increase the opportunity to impact lives.

There is uncertainty, fear, and apprehension. I, like Lot's wife, stand at the decision line, making a call on if I will literally make a deliberate decision to leave creature comforts, familiarity, a home, neighborhood, and style of living I have grown familiar with, and which fits the picture that I once had of my future and forward progress. The decision faced could easily look like I am going opposite of my goals and vision for my life, a step backward some might think. Instead, I have the exact opposite belief and I must be willing to release what is now to receive my next and to be in position to serve at the next level. It is so easy to anticipate the possibility of challenges or worst-case scenarios as we so often do when facing the unknown. However, why does it seem we don't often anticipate the possibility of a great joy that awaits in the unknown?

It is easy to get caught up in the "what ifs" and what if this is the wrong move. I tell you what… often, we have a leading, a guiding, a knowing that we must decide to heed in direct opposition of our human reasoning. I have no idea what is on the other side. What I do know is, fear is a part of the journey. Regret is optional. Stay tuned, right?

Take the leap. Choosing not to do so, may be the very thing that causes a part of your vision, goal, or dream to die. You may not be facing a risk as great as your physical death (and the reality is, some are). However, you may be risking living out fulfillment of purpose and experiencing the fullness of the joy that is meant to be yours, that you will only get the opportunity to live, if you say yes and faith-walk into your next.

See, you cannot take your love/longing/desire for the past version of you, past experiences, etc. into your next level of living. Especially, if this longing is for things that are harmful, detrimental, and against God's will and ways. If you go into your next with a heart dwelling in or desiring for that past (including that which was unhealthy for you), you risk tainting the new, healthy, next level of greatness waiting for you.

Key Lesson:
Respond with full obedience to instruction, for your life and the quality of it depends on it.

Choose to focus on God and what He has revealed to you. Trust Him with you.

An Important Application:
When your direction and purpose are clear, let nothing call you to uncertainty. Let nothing entice you to be drawn away from God and the life He has purposed for you.

Your environment and relationships are important. God will keep you in the midst of challenging circumstances, including those that may tempt you to live misaligned with the Word of God. He will provide a way of escape, mentally, and spiritually, and as He sees fit and, in His time, physically as well.

All manner of chaos, turmoil, struggle, and strife may be going on around you. You may find yourself in your heart, mind, quiet time, and prayers asking and seeking for different, for refuge, strength, relief, rescue. Understand that God can operate suddenly. His instructions come from infinite wisdom and may not make sense to you. His instructions may invoke fear within. Don't be surprised by this. Afterall, we are operating either in fear or faith at all times, and both require that we believe in the unknown and/or that which we cannot see.

The Word tells us to be courageous. Why would we need courage if it were not a part of the human experience to feel fear? Courage is not the absence of fear, it is the execution of right action in the face of and despite fear. It is necessary to cultivate a relationship with God where I trust Him at His Word and respond accordingly.

Discipleship is a living way. We must be available and receptive to allow the Holy Spirit to condition and transform us so that we release any manner of wickedness that is in us, even yet while we may live among wickedness. This helps us to recognize the rescue plan the Lord is executing on our behalf (for which many of us are asking and praying) and respond appropriately. This life of discipleship and transformation reduces and removes the risk of internal wickedness impeding our participation in the rescue plan for our own lives. Such trust and reliance upon God prevent us from desiring to behave contrary to instruction whether due to desiring to hold on to the former way or wondering about what is happening in the land of wickedness.

We must be prepared to respond and understand that not everyone can, or will, go the way we are going. A strong relationship with God, daily disciplines, and clarity of purpose can help you cope with this reality and be prepared to journey on to a land that some pray for yet will not arrive.

Let us not reach for, be enticed or intrigued by the pseudo excitement, connection, fun, and entertainment of the old life. Rather, I encourage you to commit scriptures to memory that speak to the most challenging and frequent personal needs you are experiencing at any given time.

I offer below a scripture to commit to memory and carry with you along the way and to use as a reminder when you are facing a sudden shift or dramatic change in response to faith in God.

"Fear thou not; for I am with thee: be not dismayed; for I am thy God: I will strengthen thee; yea, I will help thee; yea, I will uphold thee with the right hand of my righteousness" (Isaiah 41:10, KJV).

The United States of America, with all its benefits, provides significant opportunities to engage in wickedness. I would believe this is true of any point on the globe; however, I am in the U.S., so will speak to that environment. While there are many benefits of living in this country, there are many options for being led astray and involved in sin.

The Call for Greatness

Are you ready to respond to God's call for you, even if it means others misunderstand, will not join you, and you do not know where you are going? If your heart says yes, I encourage you to be prepared by the lessons learned from Lot's wife, to include:

1. Faith and fear both require you to believe in the unknown. Choose faith.
2. Commit fully to God and flee from sin.
3. Set your heart and sight on things that are godly.
4. Be steadfast in your faith.

While I can operate in the abstract, there is a very practical part of my being that looks for logical, concrete, sequential guidance to accomplish a predictable outcome. Therefore, I want to offer you a practical opportunity to answer questions that can be used for reflection and support your ongoing development of your relationship with God and the development of your faith and trust in Him.

Questions for Reflection

Perhaps that prayer you have presented unto God for change, deliverance, and victory requires you to respond to a warning and/or flee in some area of life, to turn away from what is known, familiar, and believed to be secure.

1. Have you heard the warning of the Lord in any areas of your life? If so, what is the warning?
2. What are you being called to release/leave behind/change?
3. Are there lifestyle factors you fear releasing so you can live at the next level of relationship with God?
4. Have you hesitated to respond to the instructions of the Lord?
5. What will motivate you to respond with full obedience to the Lord?
6. What do you believe you will gain by obeying God?
7. What will you do next?

In conclusion, Lot's wife turned back to look at the destruction of Sodom and Gomorrah. Clinging to the familiar, she was challenged to willingly turn completely away and accept what was next, and her new future. Are you looking back longingly at an old life, or elements of your former ways or life, while trying to also move toward God? Is there anything you are being prompted to release, to let go? I know I can raise my hand. It is a daily experience and a daily prayer for the strength to be all in, release the known, and leap into the unknown. Sometimes, it is a simpler process, and at other times, not so much.

Like a great father with his child, God will continue to lead, guide, and direct us, and help us with this lesson. You can't expect to progress on your journey with God and in your future, if you are holding onto portions of your old life. Trust, I am speaking to myself. And the repetition of this message is purposeful. Trust God. Seek Him, and His grace. He will help you turn away from your former way/life and find newness and abundance of life in Him.

Let's allow Lot's wife to continue to speak to us, keep watch, and remind us...

- When you hear instructions from God; right now, obedience is the faithful response.
- Don't look back, you're not going that direction.
- Salvation and righteous living is personal.
- Faith requires both feet and a full commitment.
- Set you heart upon the things of God and flee unrighteous situations.
- Delayed or partial obedience is still disobedience.
- Feel the fear, and faith-walk anyway.

Be preserved. Be prepared. Be Your Purpose.

Connect with Nisaa Robinson:

Website: www.lifeondemandacademy.com

Books: Amazon

- **LIFE On DEMAND: From Uncertain to Unstoppable**
  5 Key Principles to Show Up Confidently in Your Power to Manifest Abundance, On Purpose!
  Practical Application and Exercises to Level Up and Live Your Next!
- **Manifesting Excellence Today Planner and Workbook**
  A Practical Planner with Three Daily Practices to Uplevel Your Life and Impact the World!

Services:

- **LIFE On DEMAND Club:**
  Coaching Membership Community
- **Speaking engagements, questions, and event info**:
  support@nisaarobinson.com

For products and resources, click on the QR code below:

Ponder *I am Her*... Strings of Wisdom for reflection:

_____

_____

_____

_____

_____

_____

_____

_____

_____

_____

_____

_____

_____

_____

_____

_____

_____

_____

_____

_____

_____

_____

_____

_____

_____

_____

_____

_____

_____

_____

Chapter Three

I am Her... Leah

Seniqua Renee'

The unloved, the one God saw, the hidden treasure.
Genesis 29:14a – Genesis 30:24

eauty is in the eye of the beholder." "Beauty is skin deep."
"Everything has beauty but not everyone sees it." "Beauty
begins the moment you decide to be yourself." These are just a
few of the many quotes on beauty, or attempts to define
beauty. My personal favorite is "The best and most beautiful
things in the world cannot be seen or touched – they must be felt with
the heart."

When I prayed for guidance and instruction on which "HER" I
should write about, or who I would most identify with, I was assigned
Leah. Leah, the unloved, the "weak-eyed" sister. I felt sorry for her
because I viewed her story as a tragedy. As a full-figured, plus-size, or
BBW (Big Beautiful Woman), or whatever label society chooses to put
on my grand frame, I grew up dealing with self-esteem and self-worth

issues. Just like Leah, I am the elder sister who wasn't revered as desirable. In the early 90's, my teen years, it wasn't socially acceptable to be with or even admit to liking the "big girl." There is so much emphasis put on physical appearance but what if people looked like the condition of their heart? Just because something looks good to you doesn't mean it is good for you.

As females, we are taught from a very young age that our physical appearance is very important. We are always expected to be visually appealing. Who determines what is beautiful and what isn't? Have you ever stopped to think about how your definition/perception of beauty was formed?"

Proverbs 31 defines a virtuous and capable wife, and it does not mention her physical appearance at all. The only mention of beauty is in verse 30. *"Charm is deceptive, and beauty does not last; but a woman who fears the Lord will be greatly praised"* Proverbs 31:30, NLT.

In the beginning of my study, I thought that Leah's story was about deception, competition, and sibling rivalry. Now, I understand that it is a story about God's favor, true beauty as defined in 1 Peter 3:3-4 and a testament that God causes everything to work together for the good of those who love God and are called according to His purpose for them, Romans 8:28, NLT.

Leah, The Unloved

Leah was Laban's eldest daughter, Rachel's sister, Jacob's 1st wife, and mother to six sons and one daughter, which included Judah whose lineage produced our Savior, Jesus Christ.

The Bible describes Leah as *"having no sparkle in her eyes but Rachel as having a beautiful figure and a lovely face"* Genesis 29:17, NLT. Due to the many translations and speculations, we aren't sure what was meant by the "weak-eyed" or "no sparkle" description of Leah. I believe that the point is that Rachel was eye candy. However, it was Leah's character that made her beautiful. Character doesn't fade, can't be disfigured, nor can it be purchased.

At the instruction of his father, Jacob was to go to Padan-Aram to marry one of Laban's daughters. When he arrived, he met Rachel and was so in love that he wept aloud (Genesis 29:11). His love was so strong that he agreed to work seven years in exchange for her hand in marriage. He loved her with so much intensity that the years seemed like days (Genesis 29:20). When the time came, Laban invited the neighborhood and prepared a wedding feast. After the feast and under the dark of night, Laban gave Leah, not Rachel, to Jacob.

In the morning, when Jacob discovered that he had been deceived, he was angry. During those times, tradition was that the older sister would marry first, and sex was consummation of the marriage, which was as legally binding as a wedding ceremony is today. Although Jacob was angry that he was deceived, he still wanted Rachel and agreed to work another seven years. The Bible says that Jacob loved Rachel much more than Leah, but God saw Leah.

"When God saw that Leah was unloved, he enabled her to have children, but Rachel could not conceive" Genesis 29:31, NLT.

The One God Saw

Leah knew that the Lord had seen her misery and opened her womb, and she believed that this would cause her husband to love her. She became pregnant and gave birth to a son that she named Reuben, which means "Behold a son." A short time later, she gave birth to Simeon meaning "one who hears" and then Levi, which means "being attached or connected." She was sure that after three sons, Jacob would love her. And then a fourth time, she became pregnant and gave birth to Judah, which means "praise."

"Once again Leah became pregnant and gave birth to another son. She named him Judah, for she said, "Now I will praise the Lord!" Genesis 29:35, NLT.

God's Favor

The first three children Leah bore she thought would change her husband's heart. By the time she gave birth to Judah, her heart had changed. Leah had a reverence toward God which is shown in the names that she gave her children, but I truly believe that it wasn't until she gave birth to Judah that her reverence became for God not just toward Him. Although she knew that God was enabling her to conceive, it seems as if she believed that God's favor was to win the affection of her husband. She gave him Reuben, the first-born son but that didn't work. Next Simeon, because God hears me; however, this did not turn Jacob's heart. Then Levi, a third son, she was certain would bring a connection between her and her husband. But with Judah, she says, *"Now I will praise the Lord."* She decided that she would praise God.

Leah was seeking affection/validation from her husband, but true validation comes from God. As a woman, I believe that all women, at some point in our lives, have longed for the affection from a specific man. Having babies, losing weight, altering our appearance, or any acts of service to gain affection or validation is a lost cause. There is nothing that we can do to make a man love us and only God can change someone's heart. It took me three sons and two divorces to come to these revelations.

As I have re-read the story of Jacob, Leah, and Rachel many times, my understanding and perception has shifted. Originally, I was angry at Laban for forcing his daughter to marry a man that did not want her. Then, I thought Leah had to go along with it because it's not written that she contested. After more study, I began to ponder that perhaps Leah was a girl being obedient to her father. A girl/woman who was tired of waiting to be married, or maybe she thought that pretending to be someone else would be the only way to marriage. Most girls/women dream of their wedding day. Perhaps Leah's desire for marriage was so strong that she was willing to be married by any means necessary.

True Beauty

Jacob saw Rachel and fell in love, but he grew in love with Leah. Leah's beauty was shown in her quiet, gentle spirit and in her loyalty to her husband. Rachel was pleasing to the eyes; in today's terms, she would have been considered a "trophy wife." We all know that trophies lose their shine over time. Physical beauty will fade but inner beauty radiates.

"Don't be concerned about the outward beauty of fancy hairstyles, expensive jewelry, or beautiful clothes. You should clothe yourselves instead with the beauty that comes from within, the unfading beauty of a gentle and quiet spirit, which is so precious to God" 1 Peter 3:3-4 NLT.

Hidden Treasure

God doesn't look at the outward appearance, but at our hearts. As I continue to grow in Christ and study the Word of God, the more I come into the knowledge that because God created me, I have value and I am enough. No matter what your outer appearance, inner beauty is the true treasure. Treasures are hidden to prevent access to those that don't deserve them. As a young girl, I felt ignored, skipped over, unpretty, and invisible. My value/treasure was hidden in a package that society deemed undesirable. Now that I am an adult, I realize that I was preserved.

When I was growing up, BBWs weren't even a thing. Now BBWs are trending. There's a spotlight on the curvy, plus-size, full-figured woman. I get more attention than I have ever gotten in my life but the irony is that now, I don't "need" the outside validation. I have come to accept myself as I am. Self-acceptance is a hidden treasure. Let's face it, we live in a visual world; "looking good" seems to be all that matters, but looks can be deceiving. None of us created ourselves, we didn't choose our parents, nor did we get to decide our height, race, ethnicity, the size of our feet, nose, eyes, hands, lips, hips, breasts, etc., etc. There was a time when I looked at myself as if everything about me was wrong. I'm too tall, it's not feminine. I am too big, it's not attractive. There is nothing wrong with self-improvement. We should always be growing and evolving. Self-hate is wrong. Comparison is wrong. Low self-worth and self-esteem is wrong. Consider what is right with you. If you need some help, go to the Word of God:

"For we are God's masterpiece. He created us anew in Christ Jesus, so we can do the good things he planned for us long ago" Ephesians 2:10, NLT.

Masterpiece: A work of outstanding artistry, skill, or workmanship.

"Thank you for making me so wonderfully complex! Your workmanship is marvelous-how well I know it" Psalms 139:14.

Wonderfully: In a way, or to an extent, that is extremely or unusually good or pleasing.

Complex: Consisting of many different and connected parts.

"Even before he made the world, God loved us and chose us in Christ to be holy and without fault in his eyes" Ephesians 1:4, NLT.

Chosen: One who is the object of choice or of divine favor.

Everything Works Together for the Good

Situations, circumstances, and experiences that may seem unfortunate or like a mistake, God can cause them to work together for good. It may seem like Jacob was deceived into marrying the "wrong" sister, but there are no coincidences in God's economy. God chose Leah to give birth to six sons and one daughter. Leah was destined to be the first and last wife. While Jacob wanted Rachel, God knew that he needed Leah. Rachel died during childbirth and was buried in the wilderness. Leah, who loved Jacob with a quiet, gentle, enduring love was buried in honor with her family. Leah was always HER.

"There Abraham and his wife Sarah are buried. There Isaac and his wife, Rebekah, are buried. And there I buried Leah" Genesis 49:31, NLT.

I am HER and She is Me

Growing up, I felt invisible, I didn't get the attention from the opposite sex that I craved as a teenage girl. I was often referred to as "the big one." I would come to despise this description and reference to my size. To be completely honest, it still brings up emotions that I can't really articulate.

Sometimes, I think it's anger, other times frustration, or confusion. I am still working through this. I have struggled with writing the story of Leah because I am emotionally connected to her. I can see myself going along with being passed off as my sister. As long as I could remember, I wanted to be a wife and mother. I can visualize myself having baby after baby, hoping to gain "his" love and affection. I can understand Leah remaining loyal, kind, faithful, and being a good wife and mother in spite of her husband's treatment, because I have been all of those things. Not perfect, no one is perfect but Jesus.

I recognize the character of Leah because *I am her*. I have wrestled with being completely open and honest about my thoughts and emotions but I have to; otherwise, I'm only fooling myself. God already knows.

"You know when I sit down or stand up. You know my thoughts even when I'm far away" Psalm 139:2, NLT.

She and I

I feel that Leah's story is unfair. Even after being loving, kind, loyal, faithful, and bearing seven children, Jacob still sent her and her children to the front of their caravan in case of a violent reunion.

I am Her... Leah

"He put the servant wives and their children at the front, Leah and children next, and Rachel and Joseph last" Genesis 33:2, NLT.

I, Seniqua, was just too done with Jacob but Leah continued to be the loving wife. Dare I say, I was angry about how her story ended. Yes, she was buried in honor with her husband and family, she bore seven children and ultimately, Jesus Christ would come through her lineage. I just feel like why couldn't she get her flowers while she could appreciate them?

Perhaps, I have some fears about whether or not I will get my own flowers. Maybe because it seems as if her worth wasn't realized until after the fact. "Hindsight is 20/20," "You don't miss the water until the well runs dry." This is something that I have dealt with many times in my life, not being appreciated until after the fact.

So, writing about someone that I am emotionally connected to and who I felt was done wrong touched a sore spot. Although we know how Leah's story ends, my story is still being written. I battled with exposing my innermost thoughts and true feelings because I was concerned about how it would be received. But I have found that not only is there freedom, but also healing in speaking the truth. I was afraid to say that I wanted Leah to be celebrated and shown appreciation while she was alive. Then, I realized that she lives on through me.

A woman, a daughter, a sister, a mother, a wife who has remained true to the character that God placed in her even though she has experienced many heartbreaks, disappointments, and abuse.

Leah and Me

Intellectually, I understood that God created Leah/Me to be loving, kind, loyal, faithful, good wives, and mothers. I comprehended that God validates me, I am valuable and I have purpose. I understood and I believed but that did nothing to heal my heart. I grew up in and around church but it wasn't until I decided to get to know God for myself that the healing process began and my self-talk started to change. I wanted to have a personal experience with God, so that I can know that I know for myself. I asked what does the Word of God say about me?

"You made all the delicate inner parts of my body and knit me together in my mother's womb. Thank you for making me so wonderfully complex! Your workmanship is marvelous-how well I know it. You watched me as I was being formed in utter seclusion, as I was woven together in the dark of the womb. You saw me before I was born. Every day of my life was recorded in your book. Every moment was laid out before a single day had passed. How precious are your thoughts about me, O God, They cannot be numbered! I can't even count them; they outnumber the grains of sand! And when I wake up, you are still with me!" Psalms 139:13-16, NLT.

Psalms 139 is my favorite because all of my life, I felt like no one "knows" or "understands" me. This Psalm has been a source of comfort and reassurance because sometimes, I don't even understand myself. But God. God created me and that is the source of self-worth and confidence. One of one. Rare original. No, I have not arrived nor do I have it all figured out.

However, what I am sure about is that true beauty is shown in your character. Want to know if you are beautiful? Are you trustworthy? Kind? Compassionate? Caring? Considerate? Faithful? Nurturing?

Loving? Can you describe yourself without referring to any of your physical attributes?

As my journey continues, I can't say how it will end but day by day, I am trusting God. I know that He hasn't brought me this far to leave me.

"Do not be afraid or discouraged, for the Lord will personally go ahead of you. He will be with you; he will neither fail you nor abandon you" Deuteronomy 31:8.

I have found His Word to be true.

"God is not a man, so he does not change his mind. Has he ever spoken and failed to act? Has he ever promised and not carried it through?" Number 23:19, NLT.

Once upon a time, I was ashamed that I am divorced twice and that I have two different fathers for my children, but not anymore. Everything that I have been through, God is using and is going to use for my good because I love Him and I am called according to His purpose for me. If I didn't go through two divorces, I wouldn't be able to encourage someone facing the same situation. I understand that my pain wasn't caused by God, but it can be used by God. I am someone's proof that "it" is possible.

"HER"

One day, I saw a meme that said, "When you are HER, you never gotta worry about them" ...

I say, "when you are HER, you don't worry about them."

I say, "when you are HER, you shouldn't worry about them."

I say, "when you are HER, you never worry about them."

I am HER

Sis, you are HER for HIM.

It is written, Genesis, chapter 2, verse 22: "He brought HER"

HER, HER, HER

"At last" (My love has come along), "Finally" (It has happened to me) Bone of my bone. Flesh of my flesh. He knew HER.

HER man will know HER. I am HER

If he does not recognize HER, she is not his HER Still, she is HER

Sis, we are all HER for HIM

In a past life, she didn't know HER. She allowed him, they & them to access HER benefits but they, him & them were of no benefit to HER, just wanted to benefit from HER because she's beneficial and has always been official.

Now, she knows HER Now, she loves HER

Apple of God's eye, Beloved of the Most High

She is more precious than rubies, clothed with strength & dignity, energetic & strong. Proverbs 31 woman is she

She is me and I am HER!

Seniqua Renee' 2022

Connect with Seniqua Renee':

Email: HoopsNHipsdapoetess@gmail.com

Instagram: Hoopsnhipsdapoetess Facebook: Seniqua Renee'

PoetrySoup: https://www.poetrysoup.com/me/hoopsnhips

Ponder *I am Her*... Strings of Wisdom for reflection:

_____
_____
_____
_____
_____
_____
_____
_____
_____
_____
_____
_____
_____
_____
_____
_____
_____
_____
_____
_____
_____
_____
_____
_____
_____
_____
_____
_____

Chapter Four

I am Her... Miriam

Zakia Robinson

Family Matters: The Story of Miriam

Miriam was one of the seven prophetesses recognized in the Bible, but the first to hold the title followed by Sarah, Deborah, Hannah, Abigail, Esther, and Huldah. As a descendant of the tribe of Levi, living amongst the Egyptians, her existence was synonymous with helping the Hebrews exile from Egypt. As the daughter of Amram and Jochebed, she was the eldest of her siblings, Aaron and Moses. Despite Pharaohs' existing power and instruction for all accoucheuses to kill all male children by drowning, Miriam prophesied to her parents Amram and Jochebed that they would bear a male child who would lead the Israelites out of slavery in Egypt.

Miriam, at a young age, witnessed her brother Moses being placed in a basket drifting aloft by the Nile after being hidden for at least three months, *"And the women conceived and bare a son: and when she saw him that he was a goodly child, she hid him three months"* (Exodus 2:2,

KJV). During this time, while it is not told if Miriam was directed or proffered her services, her bravery was evident as she approached Pharoah's Daughter quite presumptuously, *"Shall I go and call to thee of the Hebrew women, that she may nurse the child for thee?"* (Exodus 2:7, KJV). With permission to seek help Miriam left and later returned with her mother unbeknownst to Pharaoh's daughter. *"And Pharoah's daughter said unto her, take this child away, and nurse it for me, and I will give thee thy wages. And the women took the child and raised it"* (Exodus 2:9, KJV).

It is evident Pharaoh's daughter also defied the orders of her father. Instead of allowing Moses to die or be killed, she named him and raised him as her own, making him a part of the wealthiest families in Egypt. Thus, allowing him a life of access and royalty. The decisions of Jochebed, Miriam, and Pharaoh's daughter were life changing. Whether this was a deliberate attempt of a mother to save her son, an act of heroism by Miriam, or an act of mercy by Pharaoh's daughter; as believers, we must conclude, like all things, Moses' existence and future was devised by God. One will also conclude this was the first of many victory celebrations where the Lord was able to use Miriam, invoking one of her greatest contributions to her family and those enslaved in Egypt.

Independence versus Obedience

Miriam, the songstress and musician, was known for her ritual singing, victory celebrations, and jubilation after defeating the enemies. Miriam was obedient when she spoke God's Word as instructed and she was obedient when she made it possible for her brother Moses to be saved. Miriam's obedience, influence, spiritual leadership, and praise assisted with pivotal changes beginning the start of a monumental movement lead by Moses starting the exile out of Egypt to Canaan. When Moses led the Hebrews away from Pharaoh's bondage into the wilderness, there was nothing but praise and belief that the Lord's Word would not return void. Even though Moses was the leader and Aaron the spokesman, Miriam understood her role from a young age, and was also courageous in the face of danger. Additionally, she supported her brothers and lead other women in praise, *"and Miriam the prophetess, the sister of Aaron, took a timbrel in her hand: and all the women went out after her with timbrels and with dances"* (Exodus 15:20, KJV). Miriam's acts of worship and praise were in recognition of God parting the Red Sea as Pharoah's chariots and his men were taken over by majestic holiness, succumbing to the depths of the water where *"they sank into the bottom as a stone,"* (Exodus 15:5, KJV).

However, the other side of Miriam, like many others regardless of intention, questioned God and spoke against authority, *"And Hath the Lord indeed spoken only by Moses? Hath he not spoken also by us?"* (Numbers 12:2, KJV). In addition to Miriam questioning Moses's authority, she also voiced her disapproval of Moses' Cushite wife. *"Miriam and Aaron spake against Moses because of the Ethiopian women whom he had married: for he married an Ethiopian woman,"* (Numbers 12:1, KJV). In the Word of God, Miriam is only referred to as a daughter and a sister. On the contrary, there is no suggestion of Miriam being a mother or a wife, which would lead some to question the reason for her disapproval regarding the matters of her family. Was her disdain for Moses' wife a result of jealousy, status, inferiority, or prejudice because of the color of her skin? In the face of Miriam's disobedience, she was immediately summoned to come before the Lord, *"And the Lord spake suddenly unto Moses, and unto Aaron, and unto Miriam, Come out ye three unto the tabernacle of the congregation,"* (Numbers12:4, KJV).

After the three came before God, Miriam's punishment was abrupt as he scorned her for speaking against his faithful prophet Moses. The anger of the Lord was sudden as she became leprous, *"And the cloud departed from off the tabernacle; and behold, Miriam became leprous, white as snow, and Aaron looked upon Miriam and, behold she was leprous"* (Numbers 12:10, KJV). The wage of sin is costly for all, and as Aaron looked upon his sister, he and Moses began to ask for forgiveness interceding on Miriam's behalf. They both pleaded to allow her to live, and the Lord heard their cries, *"And the Lord said unto Moses, If her father had but spit in her face, should she not be ashamed seven days? Let her be shut out from the camp seven days, and after that let her be received in again"* (Numbers 12:14, KJV). Henceforth. Miriam was silenced and shunned for seven days until she was cleared from her leprosy. It is unclear why she alone was punished but the faithfulness and pleading of Aaron and the obedience of Moses afforded Miriam the mercy of the Lord allowing her to move on with her brothers and her family as they journeyed through the wilderness.

Lessons of Miriam

Sometimes, we can be so focused on the problem we lose focus of the God we serve along the journey. This can be proven when Miriam begins to question God and speak against Moses' decisions. However, at an early age she took the position of protecting her family. The gift of discernment was evident as she approached Pharaoh's daughter and later sought her own mother to nurse young Moses. Despite her young age and family circumstances neither allowed her to cower. Instead, the prophecy of the Lord allowed her to move forward with courage. With boldness, she stood amongst her brothers while they led the Hebrews out of slavery. If faced today with the challenge, what would you do?

Miriam was caring, she showed other Israelites how to worship and praise through song and dance. She served with purpose and was loyal to her family's legacy. When we teach the Word of God, we teach others to praise and offer thanksgiving. Giving supplication in the home is the premise of transferring faith, worship, and reverence to our inheritance and future generations. We must be grateful for the things we have versus quarreling over the things we do not. We often celebrate and trust during our wins, but what is our relationship with God when things are not going our way? Through our trials and tribulation, we must consider it "pure joy," because it produces Godly character and perseverance, (James 1:2, KJV).

Miriam's leprosy serves as an example for all of us to check our heart posture. "Do we see the glass as half empty of half full?" Are we grateful for all things good and bad, or do we only celebrate when reaping rewards? Ask yourself, am I a connector of people or does my bias and self-indulgence separate, or impede, the Word of God. As we walk with the Lord, self-reflection is critical to ensure we are living a purposeful life. How long do we suffer from not listening to God? For, obedience is eternal life, while sin is death.

We have all been impacted or betrayed by a deceitful tongue. While Miriam was stricken with leprosy; take a moment to think about how gossiping and slander impacts us personally and those around us. Are you being your best Godly self or are you placing judgement, being jealous, or walking around with a deceitful heart?

Miriam in Me

Life has thrown me my share of curve balls and I have experienced many highs and lows. In the past, and even currently, I struggle with the feeling of being last, wanting more, and not having enough. I have experienced the negative self-talk, "the more I try, the worst it gets;" or questioning God, "why me or why not me Lord." As I am writing this, there are voices in my head screaming, "whoa, you sound like a pessimist," but with vulnerability comes growth. The reality is many of us have moments of doubt or instances of covetousness looking on the outside of someone else's life versus dealing with what is happening on the inside of us. Like Miriam, through trials and tribulations, I have learned to trust God and strengthen my relationship by studying the Word.

My heart genuinely desire everyone to win even if I feel I have lost, and I also know in my heart what the Lord has for me belongs to me. Even in our self-doubt, the Word of God tells us, *"So the last shall be first, and the first last: for many be called, but few chosen,"* (Matthew 20:16, KJV). My mother, who is a woman of faith, continually reminds me, "We are not living for this life; we are living for the next and what we do in this life will determine our reward of eternal life." The reality is our time on Earth is a dress rehearsal and we are on show. Like Miriam, family is everything to me and the consequences of wrongdoings in my life, at times, have been harsh and swift but with faith, intercessory prayer, and mercy, I am saved. We are living in uncertain times; therefore, building a relationship and creating a covenant with God will create resiliency to withstand the enemy. There are many lessons to learn from the people that have come before us and to learn from their mistakes. When I think of the Miriam in me, I must remember to trust God and that we must shield our minds.

Guarding the pathways of our soul is a valuable lesson in life we all must learn. What we chose to listen to, the discussions we chose to have, what we view, and the things we put in our mouth are all corridors used by the enemy to disturb our relationship with God. As I write about Miriam, I understand, *"Death and life are in the power of the tongue,"* (Proverbs 18:21, KJV), and you must all be, *"... quick to listen, slow to speak, and slow to get angry,"* (James 1:19, NLT).

> "Your beliefs become your thoughts, your thoughts become your words, your words become your actions, your actions become your habits, your habits become your values, your values become your destiny," (MK Gandhi).

What is your heart posture? Do you have an eagerness to serve or are you more preoccupied with your own interests and the blessings of others, you overlook how you, too, are blessed? A note to self: Your weight is someone else's goal weight, if you complain about the car you drive, someone else is walking, if you complain about where you live, someone else is homeless. "The grass is not always greener on the other side" and maybe, the very things you are asking for will bring you more harm than good; be grateful in your praise and trust God. Miriam taught us that we do not need a title to lead, we can be trailblazers from right where we are, and the impact of our actions can outlive us. *"Don't worry about anything; instead pray about everything. Tell God what you need and thank him for all he has done,"* (Philippians 4:6-7, NLT).

Family Matters/Matters of the Family

Often, we are referred to as the *sister of, wife of, or mother of* simply feeling like we are mirroring someone else's existence. There are times when it may feel like we are living someone else's dreams, watering someone else's fruit, while our seeds are diminished to famine.

However, we must remain with a praise in our heart and seek God's Word and purpose for our lives. God has repeatedly shown us through his prophets that service and sacrifice from one can have deep-rooted impact on many.

I see many *Miriam's* today... strong, courageous, dedicated, and faithful in their praise. Consequently, I also see the tricks of Satan that have broken up families and relationships caused by jealousy, disobedience, and strife. How many of us know the Word but still go against the Word of God? For us to walk in our purpose, we must be resilient in our worship and praise. Equally important, we must not misappropriate our gifts into disobedience. God has given us dominion over the Earth, with the intention for us to support and love our families. Ask yourself, am I more cordial to a stranger than I am to my own brother or sister? In Genesis 1:28 God said, *"Be fruitful and multiply"* with the purpose of building His Kingdom on Earth. *"But if any provide not for his own, and especially for those of his own house, he hath denied the faith, and is worse than an infidel,"* (1 Timothy 5:8, KJV).

Therefore, we must prioritize family and take care of God's people as He has commissioned us to do. We must be seen as believers to be a living example of God's Word. Miriam showed us when we get distracted, we lose our purpose. Let us not miss the opportunity to be believers, mothers, wives, sisters, and friends because we lack faith, discipline, and obedience.

Questions to Ponder:
1. Think about a time when your actions did not match your intentions. What was the situation? What was the outcome?
2. Do you think before you speak?

3. Are you a good sibling? What makes you a good person?
4. What do you think have been the consequences of your disobedience?
5. Have you currently, or in the past, harbored feelings of jealousy or resentment? Why? How did you, or how will you, overcome these emotions?
6. What lessons have you learned from Miriam?

References:

Why Do Miriam and Aaron Criticize Moses for Marrying a Kushite Woman? TheTorah.com. (n.d.). https://www.thetorah.com/article/why-do-miriam-and-aaron-criticize-moses-for-marrying-a-kushite-woman.

Connect with Zakia Robinson:

Email: conversationsauthor@gmail.com

Ponder *I am Her*... Strings of Wisdom for reflection:

Chapter Five

I am Her... Rahab

Engreath Scharnett

A Useful Vessel

M aybe you are wondering why anyone would want to write about Rahab, why we are discussing her; after all, she was only a prostitute and how really useful can she be, even and especially to "my God". I cannot imagine how that woman would be of any use to God. Her life starts long before we are made aware of her in the Book of Joshua. In the 2ⁿᵈ chapter of Joshua, her story is told but the initial details unfold her current status as a prostitute, but her past is not her whole story. She is introduced to us in the Old Testament (Joshua 2) but her worth and value was made paramount in the New Testament (Matthew 1:3-5).

Isn't this something that you might say about such a person, or is this something that people have said about you, or perhaps, you have even said about yourself? What a judgement call and what gives you, or any of us, the right to judge the plans and purpose of God.

Jeremiah 1:5 declares that the Lord knew us before we were in our mother's womb, so if the Lord knew Rahab, you, and I before we were in our mother's womb, do you think that God did not know that she would be a prostitute? Yet, she is still useful to God.

In a very familiar scripture Jeremiah 29:11, the Word of God says that *"He knows the plans that He has for you, plans for a hope and a future...,"* so He knows what plans He had for Rahab. He knows what plans He has for Engreath and He knows what plans He has for you. But the fact that God has not allowed you to unveil the plans yet doesn't mean the plans don't exist. If God would have told you what the plan was for the rape, what the plan was for the abuse, what the plan was for the hurt, pain, abandonment, and misuse, would you have decided to take up the assignment? Rahab had to lie to the king, do you think that this was something that she knew before it happened, and she was willing to do? We are purposed by God for what He desires, not what man thinks or says. We spend too much time listening to what man says instead of believing what God says. Did man create you? Did man breathe life into you? Did man give you Grace and Mercy? Did man forgive your sins? Did a man sacrifice his son for you? Well, if the answer to any of those questions is "no," then stop listening to man.

You are a useful vessel to God, just as was Rahab. Now, let's see just how important Rahab was. I can promise you this, you will never look at her the same.

A useful vessel to God, no one could see it in her. Oh no, this cannot be true. She was there to save two spies, her home, her family, and her life, it would all be based on a lie.

I am Her... Rahab

It was Rahab, the harlot, who the community despised.

Oh my, what are you thinking? This just can't be right. Why and how can she save two spies, her home, and her own life? This from a woman who was a Canaanite. A useful vessel to God. But what do you see: a harlot, a trollop, a prostitute. My words? No. It is His Word. God's Word that matters, not mine and certainly not yours.

It is His lineage, Jesus Christ, that was started in her, this Canaanite. A useful vessel, Solomon, father to Boaz, whose mother was Rahab.

Who was She?

Unbeknownst to most of us, outside of Bible scholars, pastors, and students of the Word of God, few know that Jesus' lineage started in this Canaanite woman, this prostitute. I know, right. It was quite the surprise to me as well, because when I have heard pastors teach or preach about Rahab, they never shared the lineage, they do, however, always reference her prostitution. Much like society today, we don't look at the backstory, we only look at what is currently seen, and we are only concerned about the bad. Although there is a reason behind everything and a purpose to everything, we don't pay attention to that, do we? I will answer that for you, "No, we do not." If many of us had been interested in the backstory of Rahab, we could have easily found out the same things that I revealed.

So much more than that.

As I stated earlier, most of us have heard of her being a prostitute but she was so much more than that. The moral compass of Rahab was judged by her culture and her community. I can understand that all too real. My trauma started when I was nine years old.

Trigger Warning

I was raped at the age of nine. I was a child. My world was innocent and my life was just as innocent and in one night, everything changed. And it was that change that would cause me to be able to relate to Rahab. I can relate to being thrown away by a community and judged by those that lived in that community. I can also relate to being an example to my family as to what it means to love and serve God and how He took my trauma and tragedies and turned them into a testimony to the testament of His Grace on my life.

My trauma started at nine years old, but it did not end there. There would be numerous rapes at different stages in my life and one that would cause me to drop out of college. There was also molestation after the first rape, which continued until I was fifteen years old. I have been in multiple domestic violence relationships and drug usage and drug abuse was a welcome relief and release from the pain of everyday hurt. Although in my research, Rahab did not have any actual reasons as to why she was a prostitute, I did understand that Rahab nor myself could have made different choices. We did not have that luxury. This path was chosen for us, not given to us. Now, that may not make sense to you and it is okay; however, what is real is that she made a choice to save two spies; this, in turn, saved her life.

This act was the beginning of the natural arrival of Jesus Christ and thus she had a purpose for the Kingdom. As far as how I relate to her, my trauma is so significant and my impact on this world for the Kingdom is just as great. You don't understand that you must endure your walk, because you are to endure as a good soldier (2 Timothy 2:3). Christ did not get a free pass and neither do you.

When pastors teach about Rahab, they oftentimes neglect to help the congregation understand the greater, pivotal moment in her life, the moment that things shifted and changed for her. It was the moment that she made a decision to accept the assignment from God and understand that she had purpose. She had to understand that her purpose was greater than what the community, or her culture, thought about her choices in life. She was so much more than just a prostitute.

In your life, perhaps you have made decisions or did things that you felt were shameful, or a disgrace to yourself, your family, and your community, and felt that no one would understand. Guess what? No one may ever understand but no one has to, because they are not God. They are not your Creator; they are not the giver or forgiver of your life. So, no matter what you have done, it just does not matter to God when it comes to your purpose for the Kingdom. Let me show you why it doesn't matter: Moses had a speech problem, Samson was a womanizer, Elijah was suicidal, Joseph was abused, Job went bankrupt, Peter denied Jesus, Paul killed Christians, and Engreath was an addict, a felon, and a prostitute. And now, God is using me for His purpose as He did for each of the aforementioned men of the Bible.

Rahab was so much more than the stigma that she was known for. She was where it all started. Solomon and Rahab were the father and mother of Boaz. Boaz and Ruth were the father and mother to Obed. Obed was the father to Jesse, who was the father to King David and lastly, David was Joseph's father. Jesus' lineage is through David by Rahab (a useful vessel). Fourteen generations later. So, as you can see,

Rahab was significantly more important than her past. She was vital to the Kingdom, although she was first and foremost a Canaanite woman living in Jericho. At that time, being a Canaanite also meant being condemned. These people were known for barbarism and paganism, a people that God had condemned to judgment at the hand of the Israelites. Rahab was condemned because of her culture but God's Grace and her decision to serve God and not a pagan god, made her useful to God's Kingdom. Do you understand that although she was not accepted by her community, she was accepted by God. Can you relate to her story? Can you?

Rahab's story is much like the rest of ours. The culture can reject you; the community can shun you, your family can turn their back on you, and even you can hate yourself and feel that you don't matter but to God who created you—you have a purpose.

I will leave you with these two scriptures, let them resonate in your spirit.

Romans 8:28 (NKJV) reads, *"And we know that all things work for good to those who love God, to those who are called according to His purpose."* According to His purpose, not according to what anyone else says.

And of course; Jeremiah 29:11 (NIV) reads, *"For I know the plans I have for you…" declares the Lord, "plans to prosper you and not harm you, plans to give you hope and a future."*

So, if His plans are to give you a hope and a future, then who are you to question that? You have a purpose, just as Rahab, just as Engreath. Just ask God.

Her Choice to Choose God and Save the Spies

Have you ever had to make a hard choice and this choice would be a choice that would lead you to a better state? A better life, a better marriage, better health or healing, or even a better relationship with someone. Well, Rahab had to make a choice and the choice would be one that would be paramount in the salvation of her family and also in the salvation of the world. There was another part to this choice, she would need to lie to make the decision. When Joshua sent two men to spy on the land of Jericho, he sent them to Rahab's house and told them to stay there. How much temptation was in that simple task? How many times have we had to make decisions despite the temptation? It was not lost to the King of Jericho that the men were at her house but when her house was searched, she did such a great job of hiding these men on the roof that the king's messengers had not found them. Rahab made a decision based on the knowledge that she had about the Lord.

Rahab knew that death was imminent for the condemned people of Jericho and she did not want death without God. So, before the spies went to sleep, she asked them to be merciful to her and all her family. She acknowledged that the God in Heaven was also the same God on Earth. After a time, it does not say, but she let them down through the window by ropes and she gave them safe directions to travel. Rahab chose to be obedient to God. There is Grace and Mercy extended here. Obedience gave way to sacrifice and Love is surely extended here all by God. Her past transgressions were of no significance.

The God I found was my mother's God, my family's God who supposedly was always there. I knew of Him but I had no relationship with Him. I needed to make a choice because the life that I was living on the streets with drugs and alcohol was leading me to death and like Rahab, I did not want death without God. So, in 2001 after I had been shot, I called my mom and asked her could I come home and her answer was "No." I was making bad choices and those choices were not good for me or my children. I was a crack addict that was in active addiction. My mom gave me tough love.

On July 9, 2001, I went to prison, which is where God decided I would need to be to get the healing started. I would choose to leave the drugs and the street and choose God, and for over 20 years, my life has elevated. I now have a ministry. Salvation is moving in my family especially with my sons. In this life, there are choices that we all must make; God does not make us choose, He gives us free-will, the freedom to choose Him. Rahab had free will. Engreath had free-will. You have free will. There are times in life that our God-given purpose may prove to be a challenge, that we feel we are not equipped to fulfill, but let me help you understand that we will be equipped by God to do what we are called to do.

She was tasked with saving the spies. God equipped her with the right house, in the right location, at the right time, to do the right thing in fulfilling her purpose. Do you not understand that in your God-given purpose, you have been given everything you need. You just have to believe. God cannot work against what you believe. In Hebrews, it says that it is impossible to please God without faith. There is a purpose and a plan for your life.

I oftentimes wonder if my life meant anything before I discovered it means everything. I have survived five suicide attempts and two nervous breakdowns among many other traumatic events and before the healing and the understanding of worthiness; I did not feel worth living. I did not feel valuable. I actually tried five times to die, five times to take my own life, because I did not want any part of this world, or my life. I could not see anything but what people had told me about me and what my past and circumstances said about me. There were moments and times in my life, for years, when I would wake up and just want to go back to sleep permanently, but God had another plan. Can you imagine feeling so worthless that death at your hand was better than life in God's hand. Well, that is how my life was. I was so broken and broken-hearted because the first trauma never healed when the second trauma of being molested by my stepfather and then sodomized by my uncle happened, all before I was eleven years of age. I was still a child. I had been traumatized three times by three different men, (family and friends of the family) and that trauma would also linger for decades. I did not know how to get from that un-healed space and so that space carried over into the next years until I went to prison, where healing and freedom actually started. Once I understood that it had to happen, I then understood that my pain had given birth to the purpose inside of me and only I could walk in my purpose. Just as Rahab.

My Why

If I had a choice, I would have chosen easier. If I had a choice, I would have chosen smaller... the easy road, the small journey, the direct path. But I felt I did not have a choice; God chose the path that I would take and He knew I would complete this assignment just as He has chosen you, and just as He chose Rahab.

My why is because I know what the tears of a broken spirit feel like. I know what being in isolation feels like, what depression, suicide (trigger warning) rape, sexual assault all make you feel like. I know what feeling all alone feels like, when you feel like no one is there. I know what it is to feel abandoned and left to figure it out. My why is because I do matter, and you matter.

The choice you made to follow GOD will the most important choice you will ever make in life. Choosing to allow for the training and growth to develop and fine tune the purpose will be the most effective decision that you will ever make for the Kingdom. See, Rahab had to make a choice, the choice to lie to the king or the choice to follow her heart. I am not advocating that you lie; my point is that in this life, we make hard choices, especially when the benefit outweighs public opinion. What is ever easy is seldom worth having. Birthing a child is difficult, but it is worth having. A great marriage takes a lot of work, but it is worth having. Building a business or ministry takes time and sacrifice, but a good one is worth having.

The Deeper Thought

Rahab was more than a woman, a wife, and possibly a mother. She was someone that had scars. She was someone who had her share of mistakes and sins. She knew love and found favor with God. Only what God wanted mattered when it came to her fulfilling her purpose and destiny.

When this project was placed before me, it had a little to do with her being a prostitute, but more to do with what God wanted me to know about Rahab and what He wanted me to reveal. I am a human vessel for the purpose of a glorious GOD. I am loved and needed by God and so are you. God is not wasteful, He is mindful and no life is a waste; not Rahab's, not mine, and not yours. What I understand, is that none of us are righteous, no not one (Romans 3:10). Rahab's sin is no bigger than mine or yours. So, Rahab being a prostitute and me being a recovered addict and ex-convict and you doing whatever sin you do does not mean that we do not have purpose and that we are not useful to the Kingdom. It is most profoundly possible that the very thing you don't want people to know about is the very thing that God wants to use most. What I understand is that my worth and usefulness to GOD is not lost in my sin, it is the very thing that can be used for His glorious purpose and divine Kingdom work. I was born in sin, I lived a sinful life, I used that life to hide my pain, and now I am healed from that pain. I am set free to do what I am purposed to do for the Kingdom. What I now understand is the greater the journey, the greater the purpose. It took me 41 years to heal from the massive amount of trauma that I suffered at the hands of others. My Kingdom work is massive; therefore, my purpose is massive.

That Part

I no longer desire to hide where God has bought me from. I do not hide my sins or sinful actions of my past; my life is not my own, it belongs to God, so my purpose is for God. I chose to allow God to train, develop, and grow me through my trauma. I am not ashamed of my past anymore. I am no longer a prisoner being held captive by my past transgressions. I am now walking and living in my purpose, just as Rahab did.

If you are reading this, it is not by accident, or incident; it is because God has a reason for you to read this book, this chapter. You may feel that you do not understand why you are in the space that you are in or why you are in the situation that you are in. God never makes mistakes.

He is purposeful in everything that He does. It took the longest for me to understand the many traumas and hurts, abuses and near-death experiences I had and when I finally came to understand it, I realized that my pain has a purpose to it just as Jesus' pain has a purpose to it. In the Book of Romans, we are asked to share in Christ's suffering as we share in His glory. You cannot have growth, wisdom, knowledge, or even love without some pain. It's not what you do in it, it's what you do in spite of it! Are you gonna follow God to see where He is going to lead you? Your past is a stepping stone to your elevation.

The Connection

The very fact that you are reading my writing in this anthology should speak volumes to you, a recovered addict, felon, drug addict, and prostitute to a business owner, bestselling author, and above all else and before anything else: A Woman Of God. Chosen by God for the people of God. Rahab was a prostitute during a time when there was shunning and what I can only imagine as disgrace in the community and sadly, such is still true today. And God still was able to use her. He saw value in her. I understand and connect with Rahab, because I faced shame and hurt and stigmas, and God still chose me, as He has chosen you.

So often, we are trying to figure out our purpose or not understanding where our value lies; it is not in the bend in our back or in our eyes, it is not in the width or depth of a smile. Our purpose is in what God has given us, it is always about doing what GOD has called you to do, without regard to what man says. Stop thinking that man has the answer for you. When you take care of God's business, He will take care of the purpose He birthed in you.

References:

https://anthemeofhope.org

https://wels.net

https://armstronginstitute.org www.biblegateway.com

Connect with Engreath Scharnett:

Phone: 984.977.0227

Facebook: Engreath Scharnett

Instagram: scharnettengreath

Email: escharnett2@gmail.com

Website: abusedbrokenbutchosen.com

Ponder *I am Her*... Strings of Wisdom for reflection:

_____
_____
_____
_____
_____
_____
_____
_____
_____
_____
_____
_____
_____
_____
_____
_____
_____
_____
_____
_____
_____
_____
_____
_____
_____
_____
_____
_____
_____
_____
_____

Chapter Six

I am Her... Deborah

Antionetta Williams

First Response... is to Pray, not become Prey!

T he Merriam-Webster defines pray as, in a religious context, to speak to God in order to give thanks or to ask for something. Pray can also mean "to make a request in a humble manner." The verb *prey* refers to seizing, devouring, or having a harmful effect on something. For the purpose of my writing, I am going to replace "something" for someone.

My Prayer

I sing Your praises Lord. Thank You for leading me to a sound mind in dark times and shining Your light in my unbelief. Free me from all limitations imposed directly or indirectly that I, others, and the enemy have placed in my life. Show me the plans that You have for me daily, so I can ARISE as Deborah did to serve You and others assigned to me according to Your will and for Your glory. I asked this in Your Son, Jesus' name... Amen.

"Do not be conformed to this world, but be transformed by the renewing of your mind. Then you will be able to test and approve what God will is—his good, pleasing and perfect will" (Roman 12:2, NIV).

I am using the T.V. remote control as a metaphor to the POWER... that cultural control has in one's life today. Most of us are familiar with how the remote control operates and its many uses. For those of you who grew up in a time when a remote was nonexistent and only a knob was used to turn the T.V. channel. Let me share a REWIND... a childhood past experience when a remote didn't exist with your family T.V. set. Tag, I was it! I was the remote with legs. I refer to this as the "Human remote control." My mind represents the T.V. screen. I can remember being called for by a loud voice full of strong emotion. Yes, I was summoned from my bedroom, from a chore, from down the street while enjoying a friend, and in the middle of doing homework. I was... just called away, life was interrupted.

I think this is a noteworthy question to ask. How many of you are "used" as a human remote control, as a substitute to a perform duty? In my case, it was to turn the knob on the T.V., but other examples included me getting a glass of water, to remove or get a pair of socks and shoes. You may have different examples of your own to substitute, but you get my point! You will instantaneously remember if that was YOU from sheer emotions that you were unable to verbalize, so you MUTED... your feelings and dared not to physically demonstrate by stomping your foot, or rolling your eyes and your neck due to FEAR of the outcome!

FAST FORWARD... to my teen life through adulthood. I am an advocate for children, adults, and families to provide influence, leadership, and guidance. My strong passion and desire to assist others brought me such gratification as I inspire others to have clarity and respond in their best version of themselves for the greater good in any situation. Often, I hear from children, adults, peers, teachers, and community leaders who witnessed me in action and benefited from my actions say, "You are wise among your years, or you speak with such wisdom." "Are you a life coach?" "Let me run my situation by you." "Can you please help me." "Can I call you, mom." "I need you as a Big Sis." "Please mentor me." "Help, please" It appeared that others believed that I had a super power that didn't exist in them. I believe we all have gifts and the Holy Spirit resides in you and me to teach, lead, and guide.

So then… I made it so. I took on the battle cries of others influencing them with my gift of wisdom, operating in faith to encourage and support them as I was prompted by the Holy Spirit. Again, this brought me so much joy! As time went on and cultural high demand increased, I was spending less time with God and in His Word. Inconsistently praying and wondering why I was losing more battles than winning, I just became weaker than ever before… paralyzed from cultural demands.

"The God who made the world and everything in it is the Lord of heaven and earth and does not live in temples built by hands. And he is not served by human hands as if he needed anything, because he himself gives all men life and breath and everything else" (Acts 17: 24-28, NIV).

I was greater in the world than I was in God, thinking I could handle the battles using my own strength. Decreasing more in God's Word who promised me, *"He will never leave or forsake me,"* (Deuteronomy 31:6)

… to a world that had done both. I was unaware of how my choices of putting cultural idols before HIM would change my T.V. (mind), even my life. I became a First Responder to battles of my own choosing without seeking my power supply, God, who is the UNIVERSAL REMOTE CONTROLLER (URC). I repeatedly continued to give remote access and took on others' relational pressures at home, school, work, and church. Allowing unlimited time and access to family, friends, relationships, work, and church without setting boundaries. Taking pride in working longer hours as well as above and beyond my job duties. Striving to achieve the highest job status possible. Doing good things… just not for the right ONE. It's ONLY in God that I am accepted, secure, and significant! I would never be good enough for cultural standards based on human measures.

My authentic identity of who I am and what I was created to do became a false identity, unrecognizable to even me. Programmed channels formed and established patterns in my mind were set. This produced a mindset reversal that influenced my values, and beliefs, and shifted my heart posture. I entertained relationships that drained my remote-control battery life by placing my health and mental wellness at risk. Mentally, I was consumed with emotions of confusion, uncertainty, doubt, shame, fear, and discouragement which left me muted, isolated, and invisible. Physically, weakened from low energy, muscle tension, elevated blood pressure, constant back pain, and suffered with insomnia. Right, all related to remote control access I gave to cultural pressures. Where was my gift of wisdom received by God which I had so freely given to others and now in need of. I found myself reciting lyrics by John P. Kee, *Standing in the Need of Prayer*. Next up – *Life & Favor (You Don't know MY Story)*. What is your song in your time of need? This is my truth; this is my story. You, too, have your own story to tell, to give an account for. It's my hope and prayer that my story will influence and encourage you who have fallen into cultural sin to fall in Love with God! Saint Augustine quotes, "To fall in love with God is the greatest romance; to seek him the greatest adventure; to find him, the greatest human achievement."

Be mindful to praise and give God the glory for bringing you out of broken situations. Seek and you will find all your answers in His Word. I surely have. *"Trust in the LORD with all thine heart; And lean not unto thine own understanding. In all thy ways acknowledge him, and he shall direct thy paths"* (Proverbs 3:5-6, KJV).

My Introduction of Deborah:
- ❖ Devoted herself to God
- ❖ Encouraged others in God's Word
- ❖ Believed the promises of God
- ❖ Obedient to the voice of God
- ❖ Respected God's authority
- ❖ Anointed by God
- ❖ Hope, Faith, and Love in God and towards humanity (Tribe of Israel)

"But the greatest of these is love" (1 Corinthians 13, NIV).

Deborah's story... (Judges 4, TLB)

Deborah – A Leader, a Prophetess & Wife, Only Female Judge
The Living Bible states she is, *"Israel's leader at that time, the one who was responsible for bringing the people back to God, was Deborah, a prophetess, the wife of Lapidoth."* Deborah's name in Hebrew means, "bee". She was nurse and confidant to Rebekah, as well.

She held court at a place now called "Deborah's Palm Tree," between Ramah and Bethel, in the hill country of Ephraim; and the Israelites came to her to decide their disputes. As a Judge, Deborah was responsible for praying and seeking guidance from the Lord. This also included her meditating on His Word before she brought her ruling to the Israelites to settle their disputes.

Based on history, the role of Judge had been only filled by men until Deborah change the trajectory.

Israel's Sin, Deborah's Assignment

"After Ehud's death the people of Israel again sinned against the Lord, so the Lord let them be conquered by King Jabin of Hazor, in Canaan. The commander-in-chief of his army was Sisera, who lived in Harosheth-hagoiim. He had nine hundred iron chariots and made life unbearable for the Israelis for twenty years. But finally, they begged the Lord for help." Once again, God heard the cry of His people in spite of their repeated sins. God anointed and appointed Deborah to free the people of Israel from the many abuses and attacks of the Canaanites. The Canaanites abuse and attacks on the Israelites went on for a span of twenty years. The Israelites lived on the street in great destitution.

Deborah – The Warrior, Military Leader, Mother of Israel

Deborah's reputation as a judge exceeded her with Barak and the Israelites who were held hostage in darkness, brokenness, fear, and isolation. *"You shall have no other gods before me"* (Exodus 20:3, NIV). Deborah's FIRST RESPONSE, her most effective weapon of choice, was the Word of God along with HIS promises. Deborah, without reservation, took immediate ACTION and proceeded accordingly, *"She summoned Barak (son of Abinoam), who lived in Kadesh, in the land of Naphtali, and said to him, "The Lord God of*

Israel has commanded you to mobilize ten thousand men from the tribes of Naphtali and Zebulun. Lead them to Mount Tabor to fight King Jabin's mighty army with all his chariots, under General Sisera's command. The Lord says, 'I will draw them to the Kishon River, and you will defeat them there." "I'll go, but only if you go with me!" Barak told her. "All right," she replied, "I'll go with you; but I'm warning you now that the honor of conquering Sisera will go to a woman instead of to you!" So, she went with him to Kedesh. When Barak summoned the men of Zebulun and Naphtali to mobilize at Kadesh, ten thousand men volunteered. And Deborah marched with them."

"And it was so." Repeated several times in (Genesis 1, KJV), God caused vicious rain to fall which created a mudslide challenge for the men, causing them to fall from their carriage and horse to their death. As God promised, the Canaanites fell PREY to the Israelites! God answered the Israelites' freedom prayer. It is through Deborah's heroine effort I am affirmed how God chose a woman to trailblaze in a male dominated role to open the door and raise the glass ceiling to serve in a prominent position in His Kingdom. God doubled the Israelites' freedom to forty years, twice the twenty years of their enslavement. Deborah became the *Mother of Israel*. After the victory, Deborah, the poet and songwriter, along with Barak, sang giving praise to the Lord, (Judges 5:1-30, TLB).

"Let us not become weary in doing good, for at the proper time we will reap a harvest if we do not give up" (Galatians 6:9, NIV).

It is clear, Deborah understood who her remote access belonged to, as I now do. God, who is the Universal Remote Controller. *"He is our all in all"* (1 Corinthians 15:28).

These PRIME TIME programmed channels are essential to add to your daily routine.

- POWER – Pray and Praise God.
- MENU/GUIDE – Trust the Word of God, His laws and promises.
- MUTE – Mute any noise that is not the whisper and will of God.
- REWIND – Meditate day and night on the Word of God.
- FORWARD – Take immediate ACTION in the Word of God.
- VOLUME – Turn down your volume and turn up the praise to glorify the Lord, our Savior… He who has done a mighty work in and through you!

Deborah's legacy forever lives on, for she leaves behind a master plan for all women to fashion after. Arise women of God. Let us walk together in strength, unity, and love, leading our assigned TRIBE to the Kingdom of ONE God!

Deborah and I are more similar than we are different. We both have served in being and making a difference, uplifting victories of triumph over adversity. Our gifts, abilities, and skills may seem ordinary to man, but when use them for the will of God, it produces extraordinary outcomes. Deborah influenced me, that my FIRST RESPONSE is to Pray and not become PREY. I will continue to have a laser focused relationship with God, eliminating false idols that appear real causing any attraction and distraction from God's intended assignment for me. JOIN me in HIS Kingdom assignments for YOU!

"But seek ye first the kingdom of God, and His righteousness; and all these things shall be added unto you" (Matthew 6:33, KJV).

"Set your mind on things above, not on earthly things" (Colossians 3:2, NIV).

Things To Ponder: Who are you giving your *Life Time* moments to while *Net Flixing* and/or *HBO ING*? Have you allowed your remote control choices to compromise your relationship with God? Has this prevented you from fulfilling your intended purpose in the life of others in HIS Kingdom?

Please review the following MENU/GUIDE of a few, but not all, modern-day idols.

Let's self-examine the list, identifying all that apply.

1. Identity
2. Money/Material Things
3. Job/Status
4. Physical Appearance
5. Entertainment
6. Sex
7. Comfort
8. Technology/Phone
9. Family/Friends
10. Influence/Fame
11. Diving Deeper

1. Who or what often occupies your T.V. screen (Mind)?
2. Are you at the whim someone else's dreams, desires, and/or needs that are not often your own?
3. Do you see and hear others more than you see and hear God?
4. Who or what brings you joy, peace, and love?
5. Where do you spend most of your time and money?

How to Remove Idols: Thanks for asking! Please refer to the PRIME TIME programmed channels as a reference guide on the previous page.

References:

Merriam-Webster. (n.d.). Pray. In Merriam-Webster.com dictionary. Retrieved January 30, 2023, from: https://www.merriam-webster.com/dictionary/pray.

Connect with Antionetta Williams:

Email: Authorantionettawilliams@gmail.com

Ponder *I am Her*... Strings of Wisdom for reflection:

Chapter Seven

I am Her... Abigail

Elizabeth Mwaura

The Power of Beauty and Brains!

T he setting of this story is in an ancient Israel satellite town in Judea, during a great festive season of annual shearing. In the old days, there was an unwritten rule where one was required to help the strangers when they came to one's gate. In 1st Samuel chapter 25, there was a couple named Nabal, and his wife Abigail. We read that Abigail was a woman of good understanding, and of a beautiful countenance; but the man was churlish and evil in his doings, and he belonged to the house of Caleb. What a contrast we see. Nabal was wealthy with great possessions. People get married for various reasons. This leads me to ask, what could have led Abigail, who was of good understanding and beautiful, to be married to such a person like Nabal? Was it love or could it be that she was influenced by her parents who, in the past, were responsible for getting their children marriage partners, or was she materialistic and assumed that all will be well with her marriage just because Nabal was wealthy?

As we take a deep dive into the highlighted passage, we see danger looming in Nabal's household. When David heard that Nabal was shearing his sheep, he sent some of his men to Nabal to get some food. But when the men reported to Nabal, just like his name, he insulted them and David, as well. David's men had been very good unto Nabal's shepherds, and they were neither hurt, nor missed anything from their flocks. When this incident was reported to David the warrior, he gathered his four hundred men with a mission to kill every male in Nabal's household. While this was happening, one of Nabal's young men rushed to Abigail in panic and gave an account on what had transpired with the hope and faith that Abigail would save them.

Unlike Nabal, whom we are told could never listen to anyone, Abigail was willing to listen and that's why the young men had great confidence in her. Abigail had her ears on the ground and I believe this is because she had crystal clear understanding on who her husband was and his capabilities, good or otherwise. She had kept her house in such a way that she operated an open-door policy where the workers could come in and feed her with current events. She understood clearly that marriage has never been and will never be 50:50! There is a myth that marriage comes with 50:50 responsibility sharing. While in some scenarios this might be the case, other situations will require one to give more than 50%.

When I look at the responsibility Abigail took, I feel she gave more than 100%, especially owning up to mistakes that were committed by her husband and repenting. Marriage is a partnership that binds husband and wife jointly and singly in taking full responsibility and liability for each other. For one to be effective in this, it's important to know one's partner pretty well. In addition to this, Abigail is a perfect example where in marriage, partners should complement one another. She was willing to cover for her husband. She is a wise woman who is described in Proverbs as *"a wise woman builds her home, but a foolish woman tears it down with her own hand"* (Proverbs 14:1, NLT). No matter how your partner is perceived, you are required to play "all out" because everywhere that God allows us to be, He does it with a purpose. No matter the conditions and circumstances surrounding us, we can rise beyond and shine our light.

After getting the information, Abigail swiftly took action. She prepared substantial gifts for David and his soldiers. The gifts included: bread, wine, sheep, roasted grain, cakes of raisins, and cakes of figs. Clearly, Abigail was thoroughly in charge of her household responsibilities, much like the capable wife described in the Book of Proverbs 31:10-31. She instructed her servants to go before her as she followed them. But having known how and who her husband was, she never mentioned to him where she was going! Otherwise, the foolish man Nabal would have cut short the lives saving mission.

Here, I see Abigail understood one of the major golden rules of befriending your fear. It is important to understand that greatness includes fear. It's impossible not to have some fear as long as we are stretching out to fulfill our vision and purpose in life. Instead of asking the fear to go away, we should learn how to befriend it, so that it is not in the driver seat. People who are never afraid are always staying in their comfort zones. It's only by taking the step of faith towards your purpose that one achieves the goals. Feed your faith and starve your fear by keeping your attention fixed on your purpose, or vision.

When we decide to step into our greatness, fear will be a companion. Therefore, one must be willing to be uncomfortable in the interest of growth. There is a difference between having fear and the fear having us. We all have fear. Courage is moving ahead despite the presence of fear. Life is a journey full of both beautiful and messy times. Any situation, whether you call it good or bad, is a requirement for one's growth as a spiritual being having a human experience. When challenges and obstacles arise, we have an opportunity to connect with He who is living in us who is Greater than any circumstance or condition around us. This is called "Grit" because it is not easy to think from a higher awareness when physical evidence is contrary to our desired outcome. As a child of the Almighty God, it is also good to always remember that we operate by Grace! The "Grace" is Heavenly love and power to which one has access at all times, even in the presence of "grit" and difficult circumstances.

Soon, Abigail met David and she quickly descended from her donkey, and humbled herself before David. She understood who David was and tapped into the divine wisdom; she poured out her heart at length, making a powerful plea for mercy on behalf of her husband and her household. She took responsibility for the problem and asked David to forgive her personally. She realistically acknowledged that her husband was as senseless as his name implied, perhaps suggesting that it would be beneath David's dignity to punish such a man. She expressed her trust in David as God's representative and the chosen future king, recognizing that he was fighting "the wars of Jehovah." She also indicated that she knew of Almighty God's promise regarding David and the kingship, for she said: "Jehovah certainly will commission you as leader over Israel."

Further, she urged David not to take any action that might bring blood guilt upon him or that might later become "a cause for staggering" —evidently referring to a troubled conscience (1 Samuel 25:24-31.) Kind, moving words. Here, we see Abigail dig into her intuition which by definition means "the ability to understand something instinctively, without the need for conscious reasoning." She was able to clearly point out David's destiny and those who hate David and by extension, the end of her husband. The gift of intuition has been granted to all mankind. Where we are able to tap from the mind of God. It is like an internal guiding system of one's life through which one receives inspired insight. When we say a prayer, we are talking to God, and when Holy Spirit is talking to us, we receive this through the mental faculty called intuition. It is a knowing that is beyond books and academics. Each one of us can develop this intuition by quieting our minds and meditating on the Word of God.

David's response was great! He accepted what Abigail had brought and said: "Blessed be Jehovah the God of Israel, who has sent you this day to meet me! And blessed be your sensibleness, and blessed be you who have restrained me this day from entering into bloodguilt." David praised her for bravely hastening to meet him, and acknowledged that she had restrained him from incurring blood guilt. *"Go up in peace to your house,"* he told her, and he humbly added: *"I have listened to your voice"* (1 Samuel 25:32-35).

Abigail invoked yet another foundational rule of Giving. She not only gave the material possessions; she also gave compliments to David which she had a revelation on! The Bible says that *"Jesus came so that we can have life and have it more abundantly"* (John 10:10b, NLT). We live in an abundant world, but many of us experience a feeling of lack, limitation, or scarcity. When we begin to understand we possess abundance by our very nature, we will demonstrate abundance in the areas of our highest interest. We'll also take a look at activating the law of circulation through giving, where we will explore living in greater abundance, *"There is one who scatters, and yet increases all the more, and there is one who withholds what is justly due, and yet it results only in want. The generous soul will be prosperous, and he who waters will himself be watered"* (Proverbs 11:24-25, NKJV).

The action of giving invokes the Law of Receiving and while there is just one source (Almighty God), there are many channels through which good comes to us. If we are aligned with the energetic generosity of the Almighty God, we will experience this generous flow of energy in the form of ideas, resources, opportunities, and people that are aligned with our purposes. Greater good will be experienced in the world as we step up in living in abundance! For us to always live in abundance, we have to continually increase our awareness of the fact that we live in an abundant world. Then, practice expanding our capacity to give.

When we expand our capacity to give, we become a vibrational match to the greater, freer, fuller, more expanded life we are called in. Another practice is being a gracious receiver. Our ability to accept and receive is the other half of the cycle of giving. And finally, celebrating successes, and in particular, realizing that in this world, there is no separation, and everything is connected. Abigail increased her sense of deserving by asking David to remember her when he became King! When we amplify our sense of deserving, like a magnet, this increased sense of deserving attracts support, such as people, money, and other resources. We must be willing to receive this support; therefore, our sense of deserving must include our willingness to receive support from

God. Ultimately, our sense of deserving must be in alignment with our vision and purpose.

Later, Abigail went back to her home. Yes, she returned to her husband as determined as ever to carry out her role of a wife to the best of her ability. She had to tell him of the gifts she had given David and his men. He had a right to know. She also had to tell him before he learned of it elsewhere, as this would have brought greater shame and danger that had been averted. When she arrived, she realized she could not immediately tell him as he was feasting like a king and he was very drunk (1 Samuel 25:36). Here, she is displaying courage, patience, and discretion, and she waited until the next morning when the influence of the wine had ebbed. She knew he would be sober enough to understand her, yet possibly more angered in his temper, as well. Still, she approached him and told him the whole story. No doubt she expected him to explode in fury, perhaps violence. Instead, he just sat there, not moving.

There is a time for everything as the Bible tells us and our wonderful Abigail understood this too well. A time to speak and a time to be quiet. She did this with ease and grace. Leaning in the greater knowledge that in God's timing, He turns everything beautiful. We need to keep on shaping our perceptions that we hold about circumstances, conditions, and people around us. The moment our perceptions shift, forgiveness kicks in. Forgiveness is key for our daily lives and the only condition stipulated in the Lord's prayer if we need to be forgiven, as well. It's my belief that to live with a person like Nabal, an everyday forgiveness journey was, and in today's life is, important. This helps us not to harbor resentment in our hearts.

After Abigail shared the ordeal with Nabal, God struck him dead. And this meant that God had released her from such a marriage! Her prophecy came to be fulfilled in what she predicted of how those who anger David, what would happen to them. David sent messengers to propose marriage. *"Here is your slave girl," she responded, "as a maidservant to wash the feet of the servants of my lord."* Clearly, she was not changed by the prospect of becoming David's wife; she even offered to be a servant to his servants! Then, we read again of her hastening, this time to ready herself to go to David. She became one of David's wives and eventually bore him a son. The Bible is silent on Abigail having any child from her marriage with Nabal. Many would view this as a huge problem and a setback. I am also convinced that the death of Nabal was somehow a setback to Abigail. However, she was able to navigate through it and turn her life around.

There will be times in life that we will experience an apparent setback. Some of the ways to turn a setback from a stumbling block to a stepping stone are to first, learn to recognize that a setback is a form of feedback. In addition, an apparent setback is an indication that we are in the game, and we are up swinging, and if you are swinging, one will have some challenges. Keep swinging! Lastly, a setback gives us an opportunity to know our capacities. Life's tough situations can bring out the best in us. Abigail recognized the shifts as they were happening. The real gift is not just to discover who we really are. The real gift is who we have become in the process. One does not need a prestigious title to play a significant role.

I believe that Abigail was equipped with being a sensible and capable leader who led her family without the title of being a leader. She ran the affairs of her family so efficiently. We have seen her being a good listener and she was a safe space where employees could run to when they encountered difficulties. She was an eloquent and persuasive speaker which she used this skill, especially when she appeared before David. We saw her courage when she went to face David and asked for forgiveness on behalf of her husband. She was also patient and very decisive; no wonder when the opportunity arose to be David's wife, she did this swiftly. For us to be effective where God has planted us, we need to assess our capabilities, talents, and skills, so that we deal accordingly. These qualities endowed to us by the Almighty God should be proudly put on our crowns as queens and kings in the Kingdom. Once we arise to our lordships under the lordship of Jesus Christ, we shall be living testimonies of Jesus Christ being the King of kings and Lord of lords. The honors are on us to arise and wear our crowns and help those around us to wear their crowns and make this world a beautiful place.

In conclusion, we all come into this world fully loaded. Equipped with all the qualities and talents to enable us to reach our purposes in this world. We need, therefore, to learn who we are, what we are called to do, and move with courage no matter the circumstances, because as Johann Wolfgang von Goethe said, "Whatever you can do or dream you can, begin it. Boldness has genius, power, and magic in it." Just like Abigail, who used her God-given talents to fulfill her purpose, she made her world and people around her better! Move, take action, and be who God intended you to be and see your purposes fulfilled.

I acknowledge the brave thinking by Mary Morrisey and the *Dream Builder Programme*.

Connect with Elizabeth Mwaura:
   Email: authorelizabethmwaura@gmail.com

Ponder *I am Her...* Strings of Wisdom for reflection:

_____
_____
_____
_____
_____
_____
_____
_____
_____
_____
_____
_____
_____
_____
_____
_____
_____
_____
_____
_____
_____
_____
_____
_____
_____
_____
_____
_____
_____

Chapter Eight

I am Her... the Proverbs 31 Woman

J.G. Ross

From the Perspective of a Wife in Waiting

Early Reflections

I am grateful for this body of work. I am grateful for the opportunity to contribute and fellowship in this manner and pray this chapter's reflections will strengthen your understanding and/or solidify your personal revelations. It's important to continue to study and discuss the living Word of God, for we have, are currently, and will continue to receive absolutely everything we could ever need from the Faithful One. With that being said, I'd like to express how much of a privilege it is to write about the Proverbs 31 Woman, as specifically described in verses 10 through 31.

This chapter has been dear to my heart because I didn't know there was a manual on womanhood. Honestly, I am being a bit facetious with the previous sentence. Quite often, the more we study the things of the world, we may find ourselves pondering where Christian beliefs have gone, how we can possibly fit into an ever-changing society, who we are, who we are meant to be... or rather, who we are expected to be. With this last point in mind, and in a modern world of self-indulgence, how can we be expected to live holy, righteous, and virtuous lives when society presents us with everything but those attributes?

As the years go by, we might even appear to lose touch with godly principles, perhaps, because mankind no longer wants truth to be their portion. When truth is no longer our portion, we come to accept an onslaught of lies from the adversary and, in turn, the benefactors of the choices aren't only the ones making the decision to no longer stand for truth. The newer generations might also become adversely affected. So, when I say I didn't know there was a manual, it is because the words of this treasured book can so easily be lost in a world of corruption and confusion.

Let us therefore consider my introduction to the Book of Proverbs. When I was in elementary school, I used to read classical books, such as *Jane Eyre* and *Wuthering Heights*. At one point, I'd ventured into *Things Fall Apart*. I even read the Bible.

I didn't quite understand much of what I read within any of the texts, I only had a passion for reading and writing. I had an appetite for complex readings; hence my choices. I desired to be stretched and taken to another level, building my vocabulary and getting lost within the pages of the most crisp books I encountered.

I don't remember what it was that initially led me to the Word of God, though I recall the pull to get lost in the words. So, focusing on the Bible, I would write the passages and seek out definitions for those I didn't comprehend. After all, Scripture tells us to, *"Study to shew thyself approved unto God, a workman that needeth not to be ashamed, rightly dividing the word of truth"* (2 Timothy 2:15, KJV). Looking back, I vaguely remember the Proverbs 31 scripture. Much was lost to me because I didn't have anyone to discuss it with. I would read and re-read, write out definitions, and try to piece together what it all meant. And yet, my youthful mind could not fully soak in the splendor of it all.

I oftentimes reflect on how different my earlier years would have been if I'd had someone to explain what this meant. In all honesty, I believe God led me there. There just wasn't anyone available to nurture or water me. Yet something inside of me kept redirecting back, year after year, in hopes of the explanations coming alive. Within my young, innocent mind, I wish I'd taken the time to push harder, even then. At some point, I traded this craving for a jacked up system of counterproductive beliefs.

When we consider virtue, our moral compass, we must consider the source. If we look to the world, then we might certainly be confused. When we follow trends or the winds of change blowing with an ever-changing nation or world, we might readily lose our sense of being grounded. When the rug is always being shifted or pulled from underneath our feet, we will no longer stand; in fact, there needs to be a solid foundation to stand on. To be blunt, our foundation can never be built on the things of this world. Our source… our point of reference, can never come from the world.

As I work on this devotional, I find myself reflecting on those times Holy Spirit was leading me… those times when God was calling me to Him. When He was trying to establish a solid foundation of who I was meant to be, I am ashamed at how I once allowed the world to entice me. I am saddened for my younger self that I simply did not know. It would take years to bring me to a point of understanding who I have always been called to be, as a Daughter of the Most High God. Yet, tears fill my eyes in reflection, since ABBA always had plans for me. It has taken this time of reflection to see He was always pulling and directing me to grow with Him. My Lord, can I tell you, readers… I thank God for being so very patient with me over the many years. He has been a solid foundation in my life and my guiding force so that even now, through this splendid anthology, I am taken back to a crucial time in my formative years.

Building an Understanding

Life happened, and I was eventually led back to these passages. As a young adult, in my mid to upper twenties, I once again began a study; this time, it was instrumental in my growth and understanding of the virtuous woman. At the time, I was a single mother, raising two young sons. I held hopes and dreams far beyond my circumstances. I knew within my heart that I needed to be the best mother I could possibly be for my sons and the best woman I could be for the Lord, and eventually, the best wife to my future husband.

Since then, my sons have become adults. I have grown older…wiser. Although I've had relationships with men I'd hoped would become my husband, none panned out. So, what have I learned about myself and how would I rewrite my vision as a Proverbs 31 Woman, at this stage in my life?

First off, I am still learning to allow God to lead. I'll explain.

I am Her... the Proverbs 31 Woman

I find that more and more people are looking at Scripture as manmade; therefore, they have lost sight of the connection to our Sovereign God. Rather than see the layout for a Virtuous Woman as a woman meant to live in the fear of and under the submission to Godly principles, they have minimized the true Biblical teachings of the passage to be demeaning to women. Society is trying to have us buy into this ideal of us being in charge of our lives in a way that cancels the need for sound doctrine, which would ground our beliefs in the Almighty God.

You see, I had been in a perpetual struggle in life. I was battling in motherhood, battling in womanhood, battling in adulthood, and battling in single-hood. In each of those areas, I was allowing the Lord access on my own terms. My motto had become: *I am woman, hear me roar!* And when I could take it no more, I would tell myself that I was surrendering fragments of certain areas to the Lord.

Can you see how extremely faulty my logic was?

Don't get me wrong, I have always loved the Lord. I just held jacked up beliefs that were tainted by societal views. Until, again, I ventured into a study on the Proverbs 31 Woman. This time, I knew it would be different. This time, it felt different. This time, I felt a desperation to get a clearer understanding, unlike the times in my younger years. In a quest to get to the real me, I needed to understand who I was meant to be and how I could launch from where I was onward to purpose.

Scripture tells us according to Jeremiah 29, verses 11 through 13 (AMP):

"For I know the plans and thoughts that I have for you,' says the LORD, 'plans for peace and well-being and not for disaster, to give you a future and a hope. Then you will call on Me and you will come and pray to Me, and I will hear [your voice] and I will listen to you. Then [with a deep longing] you will seek Me and require Me [as a vital necessity] and [you will] find Me when you search for Me with all your heart. I will be found by you,' says the LORD, 'and I will restore your fortunes and I will [free you and] gather you from all the nations and from all the places where I have driven you,' says the LORD, 'and I will bring you back to the place from where I sent you into exile.'"

My time had finally come. This began a continuous process of being pruned and prepped. Some might call it a refinement process. God always meant for me to return to Him. He intended for me to seek Him and find Him when I could handle the revelation; when I was ready to submit, receive, and move into my rightful place in the Kingdom of Heaven. (Note: As a bit of an aside, though not to minimize my point, I'd like to add that this paragraph is meant for you, too.)

In writing this portion, I had to step away once more because my emotions got the best of me. You see, before I sit down to write, I try to make every effort to submit my members to Holy Spirit. I find that in times of studying or writing, as I am faithful to Him, God proves Himself as faithful to me. In this case, the Father has shown me how He has been whispering, redirecting me over the years.

Has there been a time in life when you've cried out to the Lord asking for direction, asking Him to change you, asking Him to show your worth, asking for meaning beyond the tattered parts of your life, or even seeking clarity on how you belong… how you fit in to the grand scheme of His plans?

I was constantly in that holding pattern. I'd lost a sense of who I was. This world speaks of self-worth and self-esteem. But make no mistake, the world's teachings lead to pride. Believe it or not, pride leads to disaster. The more I tried to follow that path, the more I'd hear the whispers of Holy Spirit to humble myself. Yet, there I was, being the best me I could be! I didn't understand why I was so confused and constantly gasping for air.

I cried out to the Lord; truly cried out for direction. And when I did so, Jesus wiped away the tears and loved on me. You see, in understanding Godly virtue, pride cannot be a part of our moral compass. In fact, we must reject the world's viewpoints. And so, the following was born.

The King James Version, found below, was originally the basis for my study. I reviewed the verses and made an attempt to modernize the passage for application to my life.

So, let's first take a look at Proverbs 31, verses 10 through 31.

"Who can find a virtuous woman? For her price is far above rubies. The heart of her husband doth safely trust in her, So that he shall have no need of spoil. She will do him good and not evil All the days of her life. She seeketh wool, and flax, And worketh willingly with her hands. She is like the merchants' ships; She bringeth her food from afar. She riseth also while it is yet night, And giveth meat to her household, And a portion to her maidens. She considereth a field, and buyeth it: With the

fruit of her hands she planteth a vineyard. She girdeth her loins with strength, And strengtheneth her arms. She perceiveth that her merchandise is good: Her candle goeth not out by night. She layeth her hands to the spindle, And her hands hold the distaff. She stretcheth out her hand to the poor; Yea, she reacheth forth her hands to the needy. She is not afraid of the snow for her household: For all her household are clothed with scarlet. She maketh herself coverings of tapestry; Her clothing is silk and purple. Her husband is known in the gates, When he sitteth among the elders of the land. She maketh fine linen, and selleth it; And delivereth girdles unto the merchant. Strength and honour are her clothing; And she shall rejoice in time to come. She openeth her mouth with wisdom; And in her tongue is the law of kindness. She looketh well to the ways of her household, And eateth not the bread of idleness. Her children arise up, and call her blessed; Her husband also, and he praiseth her. Many daughters have done virtuously, But thou excellest them all. Favour is deceitful, and beauty is vain: But a woman that feareth the LORD, she shall be praised. Give her of the fruit of her hands; And let her own works praise her in the gates."

I initially had an expanded, but still limited, view of the passage. I postured myself within the scripture and tried to imagine myself, Janice G. Ross, as a virtuous woman. It was almost like me making declarations of faith without fully allowing the words to penetrate my heart, mind, and soul. I've attached a picture of my declarations, which was carried in my wallet for many years; I've also typed it out, in case the picture isn't clear enough.

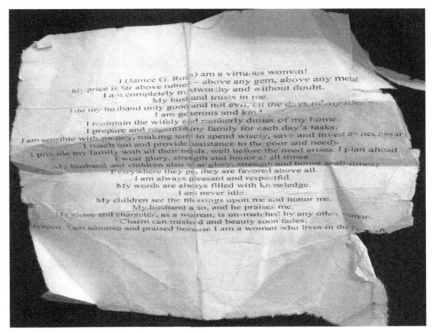

I (Janice G. Ross) am a virtuous woman!

My price is far above rubies—above any gem, above any metal. I am trustworthy and without doubt.

My husband trusts in me.

I do my husband only good and not evil, all the days of my life. I am generous and kind.

I maintain the wifely and motherly duties of my home. I prepare and organize my family for each day's tasks.

I am sensible with money, making sure to spend wisely, save and invest as necessary.

I reach out and provide assistance to the poor and needy.

I provide my family with all of their needs, well before the need arises; I plan ahead.

I wear glory, strength and honor at all times. Everywhere they go, they are favored above all. I am always pleasant and respectful.

My words are always filled with knowledge. I am never idle.

My children see the blessings upon me and honor me. My husband also, and he praises me.
My virtue and character, as a woman, is Un-matched by any other woman.
Charm can mislead and beauty soon fades;
However, I am admired and praised because I am a woman who lives in the fear of the Lord.

You might notice how surface-level my personal interpretation was. It doesn't get to the meat of who or how I am to live as a Proverbs 31 Woman. In fact, it's nothing more than reciting what we have all heard. Although it was a big step for me at that time, I almost want to cringe now. My inner self is shouting to the writing of a young woman I once was, begging her to dig deeper. Dear Lord, if only I'd dug deeper. In hindsight, I'm able to criticize my shortcomings, though at the time, I felt progress. Well, now, we're going to take a deeper journey and attempt to produce a writing that's meatier, deeper, and speaks to the heart of the Proverbs 31 Woman.

Going Deeper

Seriously: What is virtue? Moreover, how does saying I am a virtuous woman make me a virtuous woman? How can I understand, or learn, by simply making baseless declarations?

Decrees and declarations mean very little if our faith and understanding cannot align with the words of each passage. Many will discount it because they see the guidance as unrealistic. There are those who can't see the benefit in seeking after a virtuous lifestyle because they believe themselves to be of this present world rather than of the

Kingdom of Heaven. As believers, we must know who we are and to whom we belong.

Over the years, I've heard many say it's not meant to be an actual guide for living because it's not attainable. I might've even believed this was the case at some point, until I pressed on, deciphered the verses, and studied each as they pertained to my life. You see, many times, we're not going to immediately see ourselves in every part of Scripture. We need to do the work. In fact, I've noticed how certain verses and passages almost appeared to be ineffective to my life, that is, until I ended up going through circumstances that spoke to those areas. At those times, I developed a yearning and was led by Holy Spirit.

After all, 2 Timothy 2:15 makes it clear. I'm mentioning this again because this verse has been a staple in my walk as a Believer. I saw this passage as instructing me to do the work on what it means to be a Proverbs 31 Woman. Specifically, what it would mean for me, Janice Gail Ross, to be this type of woman. It's like observing someone else's grandiose life. Many look to the lives of celebrities and people making money, thriving to obtain the corruptible things of the flesh.

In the Proverbs 31 outline, our thriving should then be for a spiritual life in Christ. We should be seeking incorruptible things, Spirit-led lives, and renouncing worldly beliefs. Yet, we cannot do so if we don't know the difference. Many have a bridge connecting falsehoods with truth, where the foundation is falling apart... unsteady at best. So, let's work out this foundation.

In order to fully comprehend the splendor of the layout found within verses 10 to 31 of the Proverbs 31 Virtuous Woman, we simply must consider the first nine for context and the simple fact that in its entirety, the Book of Proverbs, which uses feminine depictions to relate to wisdom roaming through the streets as a woman, this body of work is rounded out with such a solid understanding of virtue.

Many have referred to Proverbs as a Book of Wisdom, and it's clear to see why. It is so rich in wisdom for everyday living. Proverbs 9:10 (NIV) tells us, *"The fear of the Lord is the beginning of wisdom, and the knowledge of the Holy One is understanding."* And throughout the chapters of this collection, we receive lessons in walking out this life— the areas to be alert and mindful of, the choices we make in every area of our walk, right down to the temptations we might most certainly be faced with.

And so, as we look over the focal point of this particular writing, we find a summation in many ways of the previous chapters. The 31st chapter begins with a warning of sorts to a king that appears to be of no consequence either prior to the writing, or afterwards. The king's mother is lamenting; three times, she asks, *"What are you doing ... "* She calls him: *my son, son of my womb,* and *son of my vows.* I can almost get the sense that she is looking at his life and grieving over the choices he has made. She is in pain over the choices her beloved son has made, going on to address the strength, or attention, he has been giving to women that destroy kings. The king's mother is warning about drunkenness and perversion that will surely corrupt his kingdom. She's calling him to reject the hindrances of corruption, which can certainly shatter his kingdom; to stand for truth.

This is major! Chapter 31 is two-part. While admonishing her son, the mother lays out her case by presenting opposing views of a life of drunkenness and sin and immoral women. After calling him out, she goes on to say, *"...do not waste your strength on women, on those who ruin kings."* She then addresses his behavior. How interesting that it appears to attribute his unjustly behavior to "those who ruin kings."

Let's take a pause to consider this statement further. With all we might've considered in the prior chapters of the Book of Proverbs, we get an idea of what the author was warning against.

And Deeper Still

And then, the chapter shifts to what we have come to know as the virtuous woman. Where the earlier portion offered warnings with reflection, this new section is essentially telling him, "Son of my womb, let's forget about those loose women. They could never keep you in check. Oh no, son of mine, I'm going to offer you the keys to thriving." She then goes on to dangle the prize.

So, let's take into consideration an expanded view of verses 10-31, using The Passion Translation:

"Who could ever find a wife like this one — she is a woman of strength and mighty valor! She's full of wealth and wisdom. The price paid for her was greater than many jewels. Her husband has entrusted his heart to her, for she brings him the rich spoils of victory. All throughout her life she brings him what is good and not evil. She searches out continually to possess that which is pure and righteous. She delights in the work of her hands. She gives out revelation-truth to feed others. She is like a trading ship bringing divine supplies from the merchant. Even in the night season she arises and sets food on the table for hungry ones in her house and for others. She sets her heart upon a

field and takes it as her own. She labors there to plant the living vines. She wraps herself in strength, might, and power in all her works. She tastes and experiences a better substance, and her shining light will not be extinguished, no matter how dark the night. She stretches out her hands to help the needy and she lays hold of the wheels of government. She is known by her extravagant generosity to the poor, for she always reaches out her hands to those in need. She is not afraid of tribulation, for all her household is covered in the dual garments of righteousness and grace. Her clothing is beautifully knit together — a purple gown of exquisite linen. Her husband is famous and admired by all, sitting as the venerable judge of his people. Even her works of righteousness she does for the benefit of her enemies. Bold power and glorious majesty are wrapped around her as she laughs with joy over the latter days. Her teachings are filled with wisdom and kindness as loving instruction pours from her lips. She watches over the ways of her household and meets every need they have. Her sons and daughters arise in one accord to extol her virtues, and her husband arises to speak of her in glowing terms. "There are many valiant and noble ones, but you have ascended above them all!" Charm can be misleading, and beauty is vain and so quickly fades, but this virtuous woman lives in the wonder, awe, and fear of the Lord. She will be praised throughout eternity. So go ahead and give her the credit that is due, for she has become a radiant woman, and all her loving works of righteousness deserve to be admired at the gateways of every city!"

I have made the above my life's work... my guide. Whereas the surface is now broken and I'm diving headfirst into a clearer revelation of who I am meant to become as this woman of virtue and strength, I can see myself swimming in the deep waters of all this passage now entails.

This Woman!

And so, let's explore what these verses might now offer as guidance to a more mature me.

At the opening, "virtuous" is used to offer a thought for consideration. The term is taken from the Hebrew word *chavil*, for strength and ability.

Rather than pose a question like the King James Version, the Passion Translation gets straight to the heart. The woman, specifically as a wife, is one with strength and valor; moreover, she's full of wisdom and wealth.

Can I be Real?

I am initially hung up on the fact that they label her as a wife! So, what of those wives in waiting! Such as myself?

After spending some time in reflection, I calm my nerves and approach the assignment once more. You see, I am reminded that not a single one of us are perfect, and as such, we all need to learn how to become a virtuous woman... this valuable wife will have such astounding attributes. The privilege I now claim is that God is preparing me beforehand to walk into the position of wife, as a woman with strength, valor, wisdom, and wealth.

Over the years, I've had to learn the aforementioned attributes, though the lessons were not easy at all. To learn strength, I had to be broken. To learn valor, I needed to face challenges which caused me to rise up and take a stand in just about every area of my life. Quite often, in prayer and at times when I'm faced with challenges, I am repeatedly reminded that all things work together for good for those who love the Lord and are called according to His purpose.

The woman is able to take all that life throws her way and reshape every bit of it.

Here's my final piece, which shall replace the old and be carried in my wallet. This is my entire epistle on the matter.

I, Janice G. Ross, have yielded myself to the Lord so that He can take my life experiences—both good and bad—to fashion me into a woman of valor. As with Adam and Eve, my future husband has felt the void of doing this thing called life without me. And so, my Father has decided to prepare me over the years.

The Lord looked upon my future husband and saw the challenges he was facing and how, even at the times when he wasn't alone, he always sensed a missing link.

"The LORD God also said, "It is not good for the man to be alone. I will make for him a suitable helper" (Genesis 2:18).

So, our perfect Father got to working on him, so that he would be absolved of all unhealthy ties, habits, and associations. Key to my future husband's reformation… he needed to be sharpened to know me when I enter his world.

My future husband shall be presented with his seasoned bride who has been refined and molded, kept as the apple of ABBA's eye, hidden in the shadow of His wings. Although it took time, I will be presented as a rare jewel—a diamond in the rough, a gem without spot or wrinkle, a cultured pear of the finest cultivation. The qualities which the Father has instilled in me far surpass any that can be taught by man or bought in a store. This is not only specific to me, but is available to all who surrender to the Lord and allow themselves to be meet for the Master's use.

So, after many years of preparation, I shall be presented to my future husband, no longer to be called *Wife in Waiting*!

And when the day arrives, my husband shall see me and declare, "At long last… this one—Janice—is bone from my bone, and flesh from my flesh!" He will see me both in the natural and recognize me in the Spirit. Our destinies will align! Yes, this part gets me right at the heart and softens me from the core.

Genesis 2:23 in the New Living Translation puts it this way:

"At last!" the man exclaimed. "This one is bone from my bone, and flesh from my flesh! She will be called 'woman,' because she was taken from 'man.'"

Ellicott's Commentary for English Readers offers the following for reflection of Genesis 23:

"This is now—Literally, this stroke, or beat of the foot in keeping time. It means, therefore, this time, or colloquially, at last. Adam had long studied the natural world, and while, with their confidence as yet unmarred by human cruelty, they came to his call, grew tame, and joined his company, he found none that answered to his wants, and replied to him with articulate speech. At last, on waking from his trance, he found one standing by him in whom he recognised a second self, and he welcomed her joyfully, and exclaimed, "This at last is bone of my bones, and flesh of my flesh:" that is, she is man's counterpart, not merely in feeling and sense—his flesh—but in his solid qualities. In several of the Semitic dialects bone is used for self. Thus, in the Jerusalem Lectionary (ed. Miniscalchi, Verona, 1861) we read: "I will manifest my bone unto him" (John 14:21), that is, myself; and again, "I have power to lay it down of my bone" (John 10:18), that is, of myself. So, too, in Hebrew, "In the selfsame day" is "in the bone of this day" (Genesis 7:13). Thus bone of my bones means "my very own self," while flesh of my flesh adds the more tender and gentle qualities."

I have been formed into the quality my husband now needs. And my inner makings have been perfected in Christ. By teaching me about virtue and strength, the Lord has shown me what the opposite is so I can now walk into the rightful place. Proverbs 31 is my base but I also draw from other Scripture and examples of women who have thrown their lives into this very method of living.

This woman I strive to be lives in the fear of the Lord, as such, I arise early in the morning to seek wisdom, knowledge, and understanding from the Lord. You see, women of virtue are not morally righteous on their own. We recognize our righteousness comes from above. So, I awake with a longing for my Heavenly Father. I make my boast in Him, the giver of all I would ever need in this life. Abba instructs me, making clear the requirements for my household, so that I am not idle over the course of the day. Instead, I'm making provision for the seconds, and minutes, and hours of each day.

The God of the Universe is developing witty ideas within me, so that I can build up my household in stature and finances. He allows me to see all things new. I continually offer up myself as a living sacrifice, so that I can honor the Lord in all that I do. My husband and even my young adult sons boast in me and know they can trust in the direction I offer because of my relationship with the Father.

The works of my hands are blessed. I open my mouth and blessings break forth.

It's interesting how the qualities found in the description of the Proverbs 31 Woman from verse 10 to 31 encompass many others throughout Scripture. I believe it's important to keep in mind that not a single person is perfect. I'll go further and say, not a single woman is perfect, or near perfect. Personally, I try to maintain a posture of humility and submission. I also make declarations based on commendable qualities, even when I have not yet attained the qualities or statuses. You see, many read these attributes and consider how very impossible it may be to even walk into those shoes. This might then cause a total rejection of Godly principles.

We must remember, however, if we we're already perfect, we wouldn't have a need for Jesus, or Salvation, or Holy Spirit... or... dare I say, The ALMIGHTY GOD. And so, when I think about how absolutely unattainable these goals might be, I also consider Salvation, Deliverance, Sanctification, the work on the Cross, and every other avenue our Father has provided to make it possible for me to become a Proverbs 31, Virtuous Woman.

Revisiting some of the attributes found in other virtuous women of the Bible, we can even see how their plights might lead us to attach their names to a collection of Biblical Proverbs 31, Women of Virtue. Many others can be found within this collection. If we talk about women of strength and mighty valor, we can reflect on the bravery of Deborah who joined forces with Barack. Or Queen Esther as she broke protocol to go before the king, knowing this could lead to her dismissal or even death. What about the wisdom of Sarah, coupled with the love and respect she showed for Abraham—referring to her beloved as *Lord*. He praises his wife in glowing terms. We can even include Ruth, who was loyal to Naomi, even when she had no need to be. And dear Hannah, who prayed fervently for a son. Her husband loved and adored her because of her heart posture. She was steadfast in her prayer to the Lord, and received one of the greatest prophets as her son. And one of my all-time favorites, though often discounted, Leah. In spite of the circumstances of her betrothal to a man that didn't love her, she loved and hoped. I believe when the verses of charm being misleading and beauty being vanity and quickly fading away are presented, Leah is an example. She had a relationship with the Lord. Although she'd begun naming her children based on her pain, with Judah, she offered up praise. A woman who fears the Lord shall be praised.

Life experiences have taught me valuable lessons; past mistakes have become the forces of hope because I've learned to overcome the challenges as a daughter of the Most High God. He has turned around misfortune in my life to make me a valuable commodity with wealth and wisdom. My redemption comes as a gift of the ultimate sacrifice made on the Cross.

I have learned the keys to maintaining a Godly household. I awaken early, making sure to offer the fruits of my lips to the Lord Most High as my eyes open. I worship and thank the Almighty for what was, what is, and what is to come for each day. I set the atmosphere within my home, allowing for peace to rain down.

I partner with Holy Spirit, making proclamations and declarations, or blessings, over my entire household before they have even opened their eyes or set foot upon the ground. I speak only blessings and good tidings over my offspring and husband, never strife, curses, or evil. I am quick to reject the mere thought of disruption, immediately laying all concerns at the foot of the Cross.

I listen for instructions on how to cultivate a stronger relationship with those I fellowship with, including what I can bring to uplift others. And in uplifting others, I am sharing this way of using this amazing passage of living as a virtuous woman, in spite of what the world tells us.

Now, it's your turn! I encourage you, dear reader. Using the passages above and even drawing from my reflections, how are you to walk through this present stage of your life as a Proverbs 31 Woman?

Connect with J.G. Ross:
Linktree: https://linktr.ee/myidentityinchrist
Email: author.jgross@gmail.com

Ponder *I am Her*... Strings of Wisdom for reflection:

Chapter Nine

I am Her... the Woman Healed by Jesus on the Sabbath

Hilary Crowley

Woman Set Free of Her Infirmity

T he mustard seed, being so small, could be dismissed, ignored, and tossed away. A seed mistaken for dust. This same mustard seed is also how the Kingdom of Heaven was described as Jesus asked, *"What is the kingdom of God like? What shall I compare it to? It is like a mustard seed, which a man took and planted in his garden. It grew and became a tree, and the birds perch in its branches"* [Luke 13:18-19].

In the chapter of Luke 13, trees are spoken of twice. The first is the parable of the fig tree; *a landowner tells his gardener to cut down the fig tree because it didn't produce any fruit. But the gardener responds, "Sir, leave it alone for one more year and I will dig around it and fertilize it. If it bears fruit, fine! If not? Then cut it down"* [Luke 13: 6-9]. This has been interpreted as a warning story for Christians to repent or perish, but it's also a teaching story of mercy through patience. Perhaps, Jesus is the Gardener and we are the fig tree yet to bear fruit.

Why is Luke so uniquely delivering this biblical message with images of trees, fruit, cutting down, and growing big? The answer may be in the passage between the trees.

In the Gospel of Luke Chapter 13, it is the verse right after the fig tree parable and before the mustard seed metaphor, that we witness Jesus in the synagogue on the Sabbath time of Friday into Saturday. In ancient Hebrew law, this is a time for total abstinence from work. Considered a good and reasonable law, Sabbath is a time to honor rest, restoration, and worship.

According to these verses, it was on a Sabbath and in the synagogue that Jesus was teaching to a crowd. When He observed an afflicted woman in the crowd—her affliction is described in Scripture as a spine bent to impair her for eighteen years. She was so impaired that she could no longer stand straight or even look upward. *When Jesus saw her, he called her forward and said to her, 'Woman, you are set free from your infirmity.' Then he put his hands on her, and immediately she straightened up and praised God"* [Luke 13:10-12].

The crowd may have been in awe when Jesus healed an ailing person in front of their eyes. Everybody was a witness to this miracle. All of the people who were gathered around Jesus would see her spine straighten and her body stand up. Everyone saw Jesus call her forth. She may have been ignored in her suffering for all those years but this day, Jesus saw her and healed her. May we all be so blessed to straighten up against our afflictions, and then, like this unnamed woman, remember to praise God.

I am Her... the Woman Healed by Jesus on the Sabbath

But the lesson for all the witnesses was not complete. When Jesus had driven out the adversaries and illness from this unnamed woman, the leaders of the synagogue reprimanded the crowd and maybe even the woman herself for participating in healing during this Sabbath time of abstinence. *"Indignant because Jesus had healed on the Sabbath, the synagogue leader said to the people, "There are six days for work. So come and be healed on those days, not on the Sabbath"* [Luke 13:14].

Jesus did not agree. He stepped forward to debate with the leaders. Based on the words of Luke's gospel, we need not wonder if He subtly spoke in metaphors, or if He gently redirected the conversation. No, in this case, Jesus had direct words to counter the critics. *He called out to them, "You hypocrites! Doesn't each of you on the Sabbath untie your ox or donkey from the stall and lead it out to give it water? Then should not this woman, a daughter of Abraham, whom Satan has kept bound for eighteen long years, be set free on the Sabbath day from what bound her?"* [Luke 13:15-16].

There is no answer to His question written in the scripture. Was there silence?

The unnamed woman is healed and is never mentioned again. But I wonder, was she still standing next to Jesus? Did she feel the reprimand directed at her? She appears to be the target of shaming for she was the one who was healed on the Sabbath. What did she do next? Did she run away with her new freedom and flee to safety? Maybe, she simply hid quietly nearby away from the commotion? Was she being attended to by others who loved sharing in her miracle? We don't know. She is gone from the page and invisible again.

But not to Jesus.

He had more work to do. Because who was the adversary causing the affliction? In some biblical versions, Jesus calls "it" Satan. It was still at hand. Perhaps still present. How can that be? Let's ask ourselves, who would not praise God at such a moment? Who would chastise Jesus in front of all His witnesses? And above all, who would interrupt to shame the healed woman herself as she praised God? Who or what would be fueling this all?

We don't need to wonder what tone or posture Jesus took against those who interrupted the expelling of evil. We don't need to wonder why anybody would scorn the witnesses of this merciful miracle. In this gospel, Jesus spoke His response:

Remember Jesus' answer? It was *"You hypocrites!"* [Luke 13:15].

Reading this passage in my Bible, I wondered how many times an exclamation point appears in the Bible. The exclamation point was not in original Greek or original Hebrew manuscripts. English translators insert it. Then, in this case, it may be better to ask: How many times does Jesus declare injustice out loud? It is rare and powerful. And the word "hypocrite" is a Greek term describing a person wearing a mask to cover a true identity.

This is a moment when Jesus is calling for the leaders to "take off your mask." God granted and healed this woman. Why would anybody shun this miracle? Jesus, in all His efficiency of words may have been saying to the leaders, "Show your true self."

Then, Jesus adds another powerful lesson with the mention of the donkey as a plea for reason and mercy. The donkey is the same animal that carried his pregnant and laboring young mother, Mary, into the town of Bethlehem. She would have been at her own home safely to deliver baby Jesus but, by the command of the intolerant and greedy government of that era, Mary was forced to go to the city to be counted for taxation. In every version of the Christmas story, the donkey is there. And later in the story of Christ, this same animal is present. The donkey is the humble carrier and caretaker again, bringing Jesus into Jerusalem for the Last Supper before the betrayal and the crucifixion.

Some indigenous studies, including in America, look for even more evidence of God's presence in the story of Christ pointing out that God is represented through the donkey. Who else would carry Jesus on His back? Just as a loving Father who would hide in plain sight to watch over His Son, God was there. When I see a donkey referenced in the scripture, I see an ode to God as our most intimate ally. The one who is always near. The one who carries us.

As I read Jesus' words to the synagogue leader in Luke 16 asking them to consider their reasoning, I wonder if we could interpret the question as, "Do you keep God tied up because it is the Sabbath?"

I'm remembering one of my favorite hymns from my youth singing in the children's choir. It's a Palm Sunday tradition, and the hymn included the playing of two wooden blocks to accompany the organ— making the "clip, clop" sound of the donkey's feet as the rest of us sang these lyrics:

Little gray donkey Little gray donkey
Little gray donkey, oh…
Do you know just who is it you carry on your back?
Is no ordinary load
No mean or common sack
Little gray donkey
Little gray mare
Don't hide your head in shame
For you hold the Lamb of God
And Jesus is His name.

God's presence is made known in the last line of this healing story, *"When he said this, all his opponents were humiliated, but the people were delighted with all the wonderful things he was doing"* [Luke 13:17]. What a transformation… the leaders experienced humility and the crowd experienced delight; through the teachings of Jesus that day, we witness even more healing.

All of this story was made real by an unnamed woman who answered the call from Jesus. When she met Jesus, she was small, crouched-over, and invisible. What if she, on that unforgettable Sabbath day, was also like the mustard seed? The mustard seed holds the immense glory of the Kingdom of God but resides as the smallest seed and seems insignificant. And in the order of the Gospel of Luke 13, the mustard seed is the very next parable.

Part 2
Infinitesimal like a Mustard Seed
It's the early hours of the morning and I wake to see out the window the first wintry weather arriving, it's a cold rain that ushers in colder air

to freeze the rain. I'm still warm in my bed, but struggling to appreciate the peace of this early hour. My heart is full of a need to pray. It feels overwhelming to think of the ones who need prayer. Many people in my life are sick or in a season of grieving. Many others are tackling a challenge and struggling. I'm aware of all of this pain, and in turn, I'm feeling hopelessly helpless.

Recently, I heard the wise and unexpected advice to "be infinitesimal" spoken by Irish poet David Wythe. He quoted Jesus:

"Again I tell you, it is easier for a camel to go through the eye of a needle than for someone who is rich to enter the kingdom of God" [Matthew 19:24, NIV].

Remembering this, I feel permission at that moment, holy permission even, to allow the overwhelming feeling of being small to be a sacred gift. Through this feeling, I lean into this truth of being smaller and smaller in relationship to everything around me. I wondered what prayer I could possibly utter to overcome all these burdens in my heart.

I prayed about how to pray. I then felt called to pray for one specific friend. She's a fierce spirit even with her petite stature. At our very first introduction, she was dressed in gardening clothes with her hair in a long braid. She is a master landscaper—she knows the nature of trees, bushes, and flowers fluently and she often tells me that she feels most at home in the world of the outdoors.

Two months before this, she had an accident that injured her neck and spine. Since then, she was bound to stay indoors by debilitating pain. My friend could not lift her head or sit up straight. When I visited her after the accident, she was curled up on the couch where she stayed for weeks.

She asked me to pray for her. As I did, I wondered if God was putting me on a collision path with this scripture I was studying from Luke 13. The timing seemed synchronistic. I felt grateful for this healing story from the Bible to guide me with some hope and direction for my prayer.

But it is the mustard seed, the infinitesimal, the passage directly following the healing story of the woman with the disabled spine—from the very same chapter 13, that is all unfolding before me as I pray. I'm beginning to feel the *invitation* to be small. A holy encouragement to know the power of a seed. And not just any seed, but the smallest seed, the mustard seed. The one that is like dust and is Jesus' description of the Kingdom of Heaven. I prayed with the power of a seed.

I've often told my family that when I die, I want one particular song played at my memorial. It's called "Dust in the Wind" by a rock band named Kansas. The song was released in 1977 when I was eight years old. The lyrics resonated with my heart as a child. It played over and over on the radio throughout my childhood. Through my prayer, the lyrics are simple and short, and as I revisit the lyrics, I wonder what this "Dust" actually is. I clearly see a direct correlation between the redemptive path of smallness and impermanency. As I remember these lyrics, I feel a connection to the eye of the needle, which the mustard seed could easily pass through.

I am Her... the Woman Healed by Jesus on the Sabbath

With flute and stringed instruments carrying the melody, I don't remember a drumbeat at all. The first anthem of my youth, the lyrics are forever in my memory:

"I close my eyes, only for a moment, and the moment's gone
All my dreams, pass before my eyes, a curiosity.
Dust in the wind, all they are is dust in the wind.
Same old song, just a drop of water in an endless sea.
All we do, crumbles to the ground, though we refuse to see

Dust in the wind, all we are is dust in the wind.

(Now) don't hang on, nothing lasts forever but the earth and sky It slips away, and all your money won't another minute buy.

Dust in the wind, all we are is dust in the wind
Dust in the wind, everything is dust in the wind."

(Musical recording by a band named Kansas and the song is written by band member Kerry Livgren. The song was first released on the band's 1977 album with an intriguing title, *Point of Know Return*.)

I know songs can be prayers. Perhaps this was one hidden in the 1970's charts of popular music. An invitation to be dust, to be small, to be carried in the wind. *"And all your money won't another minute buy... all we are is dust in the wind."* I hear so much of Luke 13 in this song now.

And so, as I am dust, I pray that my plea for healing for my friend may pass through even the smallest passageway.

But as I pray to ask for my friend to be healed, I remember that we are instructed to seek ye first the Kingdom of God. Jesus guides us to consider the Kingdom of God as the likeness of the story of a mustard seed, which on Earth is the smallest of all, but grows to be a great tree.

With the wind outside my bedroom window of protection, I feel infinitesimally small but now, not afraid. My prayer is for my friend, that she may experience the grace of Jesus' healing touch. The same way He blessed the woman on the Sabbath in the synagogue with a disabled spine. I ask for Jesus to turn His attention to her, my friend.

Part 3

I want to know more about Luke. As I read more about the man who wrote this Gospel seventy-five years after the crucifixion of Jesus, I learn that Luke was known to be a physician and a historian dedicated to the story of Christianity. Luke saw the story of Jesus as the fulfillment of the Hebrew prophecies.

To understand the story of the woman healed by the hand of Jesus in the synagogue, I became curious about Luke's craft as a great author of this Gospel.

In the Hebrew language, letters are used as numbers, too. The authors of the New Testament were known to deeply understand the implications of the Hebrew alphabet. So, what does the number 13 represent in this language? And what are the symbols attached to the meaning of this number?

The answer is: *Mem.*

I am Her... the Woman Healed by Jesus on the Sabbath

Mem is the very center of the Hebrew alphabet. *Mem* has meaning to include water, chaos, immersion, womb, and blood.

Mem is the 13th.

Chapter 13 takes place at a time when Jesus is traveling from Galilee to Jerusalem. Jesus is sharing His gifts and answering all the questions and speaking truth to corrupt powers. He is walking 80 miles to meet His fate in Jerusalem.

What is the path we walk as we read through Luke 13? This is the chapter named by its number that speaks to the womb, the water, the blood, and the immersion. This is *Mem.*

Do you see the power of the seed in the essence of 13?

Jesus tells the parable of the gardener and the plea for the fig tree given another year to yield fruit.

Do you see the power of yielding fruit in the essence of 13?

Jesus heals a woman with a disabled spine and tells the leaders that healing can happen every single day, including the Sabbath.

Do you see the power of miraculous healing in the essence of 13?

Jesus tells of the Kingdom of God being like the mustard seed—for it can begin so small and become a great tree.

Do you see the power of the tree in the essence of chapter 13?

In Luke 13:20-21, while Jesus teaches another way to understand the Kingdom of God, another unnamed woman is mentioned. This time she is a woman who is making bread.

"Again He asked, "What shall I compare the kingdom of God to? It is like yeast that a woman took and mixed into about sixty pounds of flour until it worked all through the dough."

Do you see the power of yeast, time, rising dough, and bread in the essence of chapter 13?

Then Luke 13:30, the powerful passage about making every effort to pass through the narrow door: *"And behold, some are last that will be first, and some are first that will be last."*

Here, I wonder. Has Luke buried the keys to the Kingdom of Heaven through the teaching of Jesus in the 13th chapter of this Gospel?

The unnamed woman was healed on the Sabbath. We learn from the story that a frail and afflicted woman answered the call, was blessed, and made whole.

And to complete the Gospel of Luke 13, Jesus teaches us:
"Blessed is he who comes in the name of the Lord."
And may I respectfully add to this:
"Blessed is *she* who comes in the name of the Lord."

As we read Luke 13, we are experiencing the teaching of Jesus on His journey to Jerusalem. We are the fig tree standing for another season. Our hearts hold the power of the mustard seed. We are the ones who are told to seek to be last in order to fit through the narrow gate. We are the rising dough. And we are the woman who is set free.

As we read Luke 13, we become aware of the womb, we remember we are water, we experience the immersion, and we acknowledge the blood. Mem. We can all be the ones who Jesus heals with His touch. And just like the unnamed woman of Luke 13:13, we are given the most profound key:

"And then he put his hands on her and she was set free from all infirmities. And she praised God" [Luke 13:13].

It is 13:13. Yes, I am beginning to understand the powerful ways Luke saved the story of Christ.

Thank you, God, for another season to plant the seeds, and another chance to bear fruit in Your Garden. Thy will be done.

Connect with Hilary Crowley:
Author, *The Power of Energy Medicine (Skyhorse, 2021)*
Website: www.HilaryCrowley.com
Phone: 603.431.6677, x311
Podcast: *The Good Energy Healing Show*
Instagram: hilary_crowley_

Ponder *I am Her*... Strings of Wisdom for reflection:

Chapter Ten

I am Her... the Persistent Widow
Andrea D. Brooks

A Woman of Significance: Finding Meaning Through Prayer

B ecoming a woman is celebrated and revered in many cultures. Embracing our role as daughter, sister, wife, mother, aunt, cousin, friend, partner, and grandmother, we progressively shift from being a girl to woman. We frequently take on pivotal roles in our families and communities, acting as a unifying force, a pillar of strength, a source of wisdom, and a provider. Distinctly, *"she looketh well to the ways of her household, and eateth not the bread of idleness"* (Proverbs 31:27, KJV). Accepting responsibility for our own lives, as well as the lives of those around us, is an essential part of becoming a woman.

There will be times as we develop into our chosen roles when we feel exhausted, when the weight of our armor begins to pull us down, and when we want to give up. Instead of giving in, we heed to the quiet voice whispering to us to seek God, and kneel and pray for strength, help, wisdom, courage, healing, clarity, and peace. For HE is the source of our strength and wants to take care of us as we are HIS daughters. As we are reminded in Numbers 6:24, GNT: *"May the Lord bless you and take care of you."*

In our clarity, the will to continue on toward our purpose becomes evident, similarly like the parable of *The Persistent Widow*. This unique woman serves as a representation for the kind of resilience all women have experienced at some point in their life. She never gave up and relied on her courage to obtain justice. Like her, you and I have attempted to figure out ways to triumph over adversity. This will always be true because a godly woman never gives up, *"the name of the Lord is a strong fortress; the godly run to him and are safe"* (Proverbs 18:10 NLT).

The Parable of The Persistent Widow

In the Gospel of Luke, Jesus tells numerous parables to help His followers become more spiritual and to inspire nonbelievers. In particular, Jesus shared the parable of The Persistent Widow (Luke 18: 1-8) to His disciples to remind them that they should remain steadfast with their prayers and to never give up. Interestingly, despite being a story delivered to males, Jesus uses the example of a widowed woman, who was perceived to be weak during biblical times, to demonstrate his teaching of praying diligently and never giving up. In 1 Corinthians 1:27 (NLT), we are reminded that *"God chose things the world considers foolish in order to shame those who think they are wise. And he chose things that are powerless to shame those who are powerful."*

Our sister sought justice from an earthly man who did not fear God and who continuously turned her away, but each time she returned with courage, reiterating her request. We are reminded that *"she is clothed with strength and dignity, and she laughs without fear of the future"* (Proverbs 31:25, NLT). Although her insistence was admirable, it is important to remember that we are to seek God because everything comes from HIM *"for although the first woman came from man, every other man was born from a woman, and everything comes from God"* (1 Corinthians 11:12, NLT). During this season of hardship in her life, she relentlessly asked the unjust judge to *"grant me justice against my adversary"* (Luke 18:3, NIV) until he finally granted her request. The unjust judge states, *"but this woman is driving me crazy. I'm going to see that she gets justice, because she is wearing me out with her constant requests!"* (Luke 18:5, NLT). Her perseverance paid off as she fearlessly sought what she thought was best for her. She may have been afraid, but she didn't let fear deter her. For it is written, *"This is my command, be strong and courageous! Do not be afraid or discouraged. For the LORD your God is with you wherever you go"* (Joshua 1:9, NIV).

Can you remember a time when you were focused on a particular outcome and had to keep seeking help from someone who didn't want to help you? How did it make you feel? Did you find the strength to keep going? The concept of divine omniscience is exemplified in the narrative of the persistent widow, which imparts the significance of unwavering determination during challenging circumstances, as it underscores the notion that no task is insurmountable until its completion. Jesus wanted His disciples to never give up in praying and remain faithful because He may have been preparing them for the road ahead. Remaining focused during the storms of life require us to hold on to God's promises and never turn our back on praying because if we do, doubt and worry will sow seeds of confusion, stress, and distraction. In short, a final word: *"Be strong in the Lord and in his mighty power. Put on all of God's armor so that you will be able to stand firm against all the strategies of the devil"* (Ephesians 6: 10-11, NLT).

Our sister, The Persistent Widow, is described as persistent, which also means resilient, determined, tenacious, insistent. You, woman of God, are powerful just as our sister widow!

Women & Identity

In the different seasons of your life, how do you identify as a woman of God? You are constantly evolving and adapting as you experience life. Are you seeking God during this time? Is He seeking you? Over the years, I have read a variety of self-care books, devotionals, magazines, and at times, the Bible, to help me understand my journey. Specifically, I can remember a time when my emotions were out of control, and I didn't know who I wanted to be. In my quest for self-understanding, I discovered *Acts of Faith* by Iyanla Vanzant and read the daily devotional readings for self-discovery. Particularly, one devotional I gravitated towards posed two questions: "How do you start your day?" and "Who are you?" These two questions were influential in my life for a period of time. When I reflect on my past, my inflexibility, irresponsible choices, and insecurity were driving forces to push me on the path of getting to know God. How did I do this? By starting my day talking to God *"and we know that God caused everything to work together for the good of those who love God and are called according to this purpose for them"* (Romans 8:28, NLT).

A fundamental characteristic of The Persistent Widow's identity is her perseverance and position to remain steadfast during this difficult time, which could have broken her spirit. She decided who she was, was enough to make it through her hardship. *"God is in the midst of her; she will not be moved; God will help her when the morning dawns"* (Psalm 46:5, AMP). How has the strength of your identity led you to deal with challenging encounters in your life?

I believe God led me to write about The Persistent Widow in order to shed light on her significance and the parallels between her life and the lives of all women. Prayer can help you remain centered during difficult times because you can ask God for what you need. *"For everyone who asks will receive, and anyone who seeks will find, and the door will be opened to those who knock"* (Matthew 7:7-8, GNT). Prayer is communication with God and asking for what you believe is important, however, even though you ask, seek, and knock, God's plan isn't always the same as ours. His wisdom and knowledge surpass our understanding and He will guide us and make our paths clear. *"For I know the plans I have for you," says the LORD. 'They are plans for good and not for disaster to give you a future and a hope"* (Jeremiah 29:11, NLT).

Deciding how you identify with this incredible woman can lead toward your self-authenticity. We are alive and constantly making decisions, learning from mistakes, encountering defeats, walking through valleys, and climbing mountains. We are also experiencing joys, creating memorable moments, celebrating accomplishments, feeling, giving, and receiving love. Without these transformational experiences, would we know God's will for us and how amazing HE is? *"Don't copy the behavior and customs of this world, but let God transform you into a new person by changing the way you think. Then you will learn to know God's will for you, which is good and pleasing and perfect"* (Romans 12:2, NLT).

Therefore, in the face of adversity, one must exhibit the great moral quality of perseverance in order to bring about the necessary transformation. There is honor in our commitment to move forward when we are too tired, too frustrated, too overwhelmed, and too discouraged. Remembering that our fortitude comes from the power of God's Spirit, who is the source of our strength is vital. *"But they that wait upon the LORD shall renew their strength; they shall mount up with wings as eagles; they shall run, and not be weary; and they shall walk, and not faint"* (Isaiah 40:31, KJV).

The Persistent Widow persisted. I am persisting. You are persisting. Repeat aloud: *I AM HER* because SHE is ME, and I AM a WOMAN.

"But a woman that feareth the LORD she shall be praised"(Proverbs 31:30, KJV).

Heart of a Woman

"As a face is reflected in water, so the heart reflects the real person" (Proverbs 27:19, NLT).

Our heart, both physically and emotionally, is a necessity for us to live. It is central to our body and the muscle that stimulates the sustenance of life to flow throughout our body. Our heart unifies our mind, body, and soul and allows us to experience emotion, which is also central to our identity. Spiritually, the heart represents strength and is the center of our relationship with God. It unifies our mind, body, and soul which allows us to feel affection. In Mark 12:30 (CSB), Jesus instructed us to *"love the Lord your God with all your heart, with all your soul, with all your mind, and with all your strength."*

Our narrow capacity to understand and accept God's intention for our lives and the peace that comes from relying on Him alone is either strengthened or weakened by the difficulties in our lives. Our sister was in distress and knew what she needed and forged forward despite the risks. Life is going to happen, unexpected stresses, health concerns, anxiety, financial setbacks, parenting blunders, you name it, it may happen. The key is, remembering Jesus's teaching to *"pray and never give up"* (Luke 18:1, NLT). In praying, we can find serenity that only God can provide to help us through life. *"For he himself is our peace"* (Ephesians 2:14, NIV). I wonder if our sister widow prayed, if she was led because of her heart posture toward God. Our hearts know that God is all-encompassing, and our resilience emanates from our spirit, and our steadfastness relies on the solid ground of our unwavering faith in God. When faced with difficulties, turn to God and His heartfelt promises to help you endure them as the scripture states, *"Jesus looked at them intently and said, "Humanly speaking, it is impossible. But with God everything is possible"* (Matthew 19:26, KJV). Could it be Jesus knew the strength of a woman? Just as our sister, The Persistent Widow, didn't give up, neither should you for God is with you!

Remain Faithful

I remember learning snippets about faith here and there during my childhood and teenage years; however, I was still struggling to understand the concept of faith as a young woman. Jesus ends the Parable of The Persistent Widow asking this question: *"However, when the Son of Man comes, will he find faith on the earth?"* (Luke 18:8, NIV). Where are you in your faith walk? God is aware of every tear we cry, of the days we are worn out, irritated, and eager for a change; nonetheless, He wants us to pray to Him and keep the faith! *"The Lord will fight for you; you need only to be still"* (Exodus 14:14, NIV).

There was a time in my life when I worked at a job for seven years despite feeling that I had outgrown it. After three years, I had reached my lowest point. I looked for work at other universities, but nothing developed. During my fourth year, I was offered a new employment opportunity and accepted, but something unusual occurred during the hiring process and the offer was suddenly withdrawn. I was exhausted, angry, and unhappy and just wanted to leave, but I needed the job for my livelihood. At some point, I accepted it wasn't my time to leave and instead, I prayed and waited for God. In the meantime, I sought to change my negative outlook into an optimistic one, focusing on gratitude and all that God had provided in my life, including my job. *"Let us not become weary in doing good for at the proper time we will reap a harvest if we do not give up"* (Galatians 6:9, NIV).

Unbeknownst to me, God was actually preparing my new journey into motherhood! I was very clear on my intention of wanting to stay home with my son for the first year of his life. My delivery date was soon approaching, and I didn't have a concrete financial plan to support my decision. I believe God puts earthly angels in our lives to remind us that He is with us. I became very close with a woman who reminded me of my paternal grandmother, she had a gentle, spiritual strength. She sensed my worry and I distinctively remember her sharing Philippians 4:4-7 (NIV) with me: *"Do not be anxious about anything; but in every situation, by prayer and petition, with thanksgiving, present your requests to God. And the peace of God, which transcends all understanding, will guard your hearts and your minds in Christ Jesus."*

About three weeks before my delivery date, my employer made organizational changes and my department would be downsizing with my last day quickly approaching. I am reminded that "God is not human that he should lie, not a human being, that he should change his mind. Does he speak and then not act? Does he promise and not fulfill?" (Numbers 23:19, NIV). Needless to say, I was thrilled! *"Rejoice always!"* (1Thessalonians 5:16, NIV). In hindsight, I learned many lessons; one of which is that God will fix it in His time because He is a way maker, HE is Jehovah Jireh, our provider, and the sustainer of our life. Had I left my job when I wanted, I would not have received an adequate severance package, which provided the financial means to stay home with my son. *"He will never leave you nor forsake you"* (Deuteronomy 31:8, NIV).

To be diligent with prayer is the reason Jesus taught the parable of The Persistent Widow. *"Pray Continually"* (1Thessalonians 5:17, NIV). Therefore, women of God, when circumstances are tough, when it seems hopeless, PRAY to God, and remain faithful because He is able. The will of God will never take you where the grace of God cannot sustain you. God hasn't forgotten you or your prayers! Can you imagine how alone or afraid our sister was as she had to ask the judge for help? Can you remember times when you wanted something but were afraid? The core of remaining faithful is thanking God in advance. *"Therefore, I say unto you, what things soever ye desire, when ye pray, believe that ye receive them, and ye shall have them"* (Mark 11:24, KJV). And when God does answer your prayers, thank HIM, and praise HIM for blessing you because HE deserves all the glory and honor. *"And in the midst of everything, be always giving thanks, for this is God's perfect plan for you in Christ Jesus"* (1Thessalonians 5:18, TPT).

Prayers and Blessings
"Every good gift and every perfect gift is from above, and cometh down from the Father of lights, with whom is no variableness, neither shadow of turning" (James 1:17, KJV).

Look around and count your blessings. Yup, that's one. There's another. Do you notice them? Keep counting. I know, I get it, things are not what you want now; remember, your current blessings are previously answered prayers. Do you remember when you prayed for what you have now? The purpose of God's blessings is to provide you with hope and to recognize His favor in your life. *"The Lord bless you and keep you; the Lord make his face shine upon you and be gracious to you; the Lord turn his face toward you and give you peace"* (Numbers 6: 24-26, NIV).

Start each day with a grateful heart and focus on positive intentionality. Life is going to happen, things occur out of our control, but how will you respond? How did the persistent widow respond? With grace and consistency, and so can you! Feeling angry, seek Him; feeling unfulfilled, seek Him; feeling unloved, seek Him; feeling worried, seek Him; feeling discouraged, seek Him; feeling lonely, seek Him. God promises to guide and reveal marvelous things to us if we seek Him. "And Jesus looking upon them saith, *"With men it is impossible, but not with God: for with God all things are possible"* (Mark 10:27, KJV).

We don't know what our sister widow used to fuel her motivation; however, you have the opportunity to recharge. Meditate on your favorite scriptures, listen to praise and worship music, search for God's promises and post them on your bathroom mirror, write them in your journal, commit them to memory as we are sustainable by the sustenance of HIS Word. *"Worry weighs a person down; an encouraging word cheers a person up"* (Proverbs 12:25, NLT).

Pray and Wait

Patience is a virtue and requires us to remain calm and endure. I'm not sure about you, but I have never been a patient person. I've prayed time and time again asking God to give me patience, always waiting for patience until I realized after each setback to demonstrate patience, God was injecting me into situations where I had to exercise my patience muscle. But her patience led to her resilience, which was manifested in her justness to receive her justice. *"And will not God bring about justice for his chosen ones, who cry out to him day and night? "I tell you he will see that they get justice, and quickly"* (Luke 18:7-8, NIV).

Pray and wait. Use this time to reflect on the Positive P's: Patience, Persistence, and Promises, gifts from God to sustain you while you wait to hear from Him. *"Trust in the LORD with all of your heart and lean not on your own understanding; in all of your ways submit to him, and he will make your paths straight"* (Proverbs 3:5-6, NIV). Furthermore, in Matthew 6:34 (NIV), it is written: *"Therefore, do not worry about tomorrow, for tomorrow will worry about itself. Each day has enough trouble of its own."*

Women and Inspiration

Our sister widow is an inspiration because of her resilience. The judge in this parable *"who neither feared God nor cared about people"* (Luke 18:2, NIV), ended up giving our sister what she wanted because he was weary of her resilience. Day after day, she kept at it because she knew that this was the only way to find relief from her adversary. Her persistence is our inspiration to *"Do everything without complaining and arguing, so that no one can criticize you. Live clean, innocent lives as children of God, shining like bright lights in a world full of crooked and perverse people"* (Philippians 2:14-15, NLT).

When it comes to women and inspiration, I previously mentioned my belief of God in placing earthly angels in our life for spiritual support.

Who are the earthly angels that God has placed in your life? Women who symbolize similarities of The Persistent Widow.

God led me to a group of dynamic women who were studying the Book of Proverbs and once completed, we committed to reading and studying the Book of Psalm. This was such a pivotal time in my life because in studying God's Word, I was inspired by the unwavering faith of these ladies. And even though there were a few men who popped in to share their wisdom, it was the strength of our womanhood anchored in God's infinite wisdom that allowed us to cross paths, connect, and inspire each other. *"Let us think of ways to motivate one another to acts of love and good works"* (Hebrews 10:24, NLT).

The Persistent Widow was a woman of resolve, a prominent woman all women can relate to. I believe through His teaching, Jesus illustrated the strength, beauty, and heart of a woman. In the midst your storm, remember, God will be there with you every step of the way for it is written: *"Do not fear, for I have redeemed you; I have summoned you by name; you are mine. When you pass through the waters, I will be with you; and through the rivers, they shall not sweep over you. When you walk through the fire, you will not be burned; the flames will not set you ablaze. For I am the LORD your God, the Holy One of Israel, your Savior"* (Isaiah 43:1-3, NIV).

Woman of God, my prayer is that you are aware of God's strength within you and your capability to persevere in the face of adversity. Digging deep and overcoming is what we do! So, regardless of where you are in life right now, I pray that you have a deeper understanding of God's love for you because of our sister, The Persistent Widow. I hope this significant woman has inspired you as much as she has me! May you continue to pray with diligence and consistency, so that you understand the meaning of God in your life. May God's peace and grace always be with you.

Contact Andrea D. Brooks:

Email: brooksad132@gmail.com

Ponder *I am Her*... Strings of Wisdom for reflection:

_____
_____
_____
_____
_____
_____
_____
_____
_____
_____
_____
_____
_____
_____
_____
_____
_____
_____
_____
_____
_____
_____
_____
_____
_____
_____

Chapter Eleven

I am Her... the Woman at the Well

Siobhan B.

In Spirit and Truth, John 4

Here I humbly share my learnings and discoveries through John 4 and the Samaritan Woman. I am deeply grateful for the creation of this project through my beautiful sister, Nycholle Woolfolk-Gater, who has initiated and led the way for this project when the Lord asked her to share the stories of the Women of the Bible. So many times, growing up, I longed for a greater connection with, and representation of, women in the Bible, particularly in the way it was spoken of and taught to me. Through this project, I have discovered many incredible women and stories that I had previously had a limited perception of. I pray that these chapters awaken in you a greater representation, connection, and discovery of these magnificent Women of the Bible.

Maybe, you are very familiar with the Samaritan Woman in John 4 and my revelations and learnings will be very common for you. Maybe, you are new to the Bible, and this passage will cause you to discover new aspects of Scripture. I myself, having known of this passage for decades, now see it anew. The learnings have been full of revelations for me, and in all honesty, at times, rather uncomfortable as God shows me with grace and love (as Jesus did in this passage with the Samaritan woman), all the ways in which I had forgotten or turned from my truest self and now, I am able to see more clearly through God's/Jesus' unconditional love.

The Messiah

Jesus reveals in this passage that He is the Messiah, Jesus Christ:

"The woman said to Him, "I know that Messiah is coming" (who is called Christ). "When He comes, He will tell us all things." Jesus said to her, "I who speak to you am He" (John 4:25, NKJV).

Jesus, choosing to share that He is the Messiah with the Samaritan woman, indicates how significant this passage is. The people have known a Messiah is coming and to finally have this revealed to them is a monumental moment. As always, this passage does not only reveal that Jesus is the Messiah, but it is also layered with lessons, insights, and profound perspective. Truthfully, I hadn't realized until I sat, prayed, and lived with this text for these months just how much is shared with us in John 4. To begin touching upon the richness of this chosen timing, let's take a moment to look at John 3.

In John 3, Jesus was with a man of the Pharisees named Nicodemus, a ruler of the Jews (John 3:1, NKJV), if Jesus' motivation were solely to spread the Word far and wide that He is Christ the Messiah, He could have done so through Nicodemus; however, it is in John 4 where we discover the divine timing that Jesus shares that He is Christ. Let's dive deeper into this divine timing and its blessings for our lives.

The Samaritan Woman

The Samaritan woman without a name. So frequently as a child, I took offence and felt disregarded as a female in my understanding of and the ways I was taught about the women in the Bible. Having worked on this project, so much healing has taken place. I now feel that referring to this woman as the *'Samaritan woman'* rather than giving her name, allows the focus to remain on what she represents and how she is a part of all of us, rather than separate or superior to us. It also represents a fundamental change in the way that Jesus is teaching us we must worship. Referring to her as the *'Samaritan woman'* was never to undermine her value; instead, it shines a light on how significant her role is in the Messiah being revealed to the people and the new way we must worship with God.

Then, the woman of Samaria said to Him, *"How is it that You, being a Jew, ask a drink from me, a Samaritan woman?" For Jews have no dealings with Samaritans"* (John 4:9, NKJV).

The words *'Samaritan woman'* may not hold much significance nowadays; however in those times, there was a large racial prejudice between the Jews and the Samaritans. The Samaritans were seen as an undesirable mixed race who Jews wouldn't associate with or even share dishes with (hence the significance of Jesus, a Jew, asking for a drink without His own container/vessel). As well as being a Samaritan, she is also a woman, it was shocking in those times for a man to be alone with a woman talking with her, especially as she was deemed to be living in sin, having had five husbands, and the one whom you now have is not your husband (John 4:18, NKJV). Here, Jesus goes beyond prejudice based on race, religion, gender, and societal barriers/condemnation, connecting with the truth of the person, and spirit before Him.

What societal barriers do you notice in your life? How do you feel condemned, or in what ways do you condemn or separate yourself from others? Notice what comes up for you in response to those questions as we journey deeper into the lessons John 4 offers us. How does it feel to know that Jesus has intentionally chosen to connect with a person of a different race, gender, religious belief, and an outcast, that others have looked down on? What does this represent or teach you about the true embodiment of Christ consciousness in your own life?

The Route

Jesus left Judea and departed again to Galilee. But He needed to go through Samaria (John 4:3-4, NKJV). It was common for Jews traveling to take a much longer route to Galilee to avoid Samaria and the Samaritans who lived there; however, Jesus chose to go through Samaria and the city of Sychar where Samaritans lived (people who were judged and condemned by Jews). Throughout the stories of Jesus, we see how He reaches out to the 'sinners,' outcasts, and forgotten ones. For Jesus to reveal He is Christ to a Samaritan, whom is also a woman and an outcast of her society, signifies how Jesus loves us beyond any judgements, limitations, or sin, breaking boundaries through His work with God. Jesus truly redefines what it is to love your neighbor.

It says that He needed to go through Samaria (John 4:4, NKJV). It is less common to hear of Jesus 'needing' something; this signifies how important it was, at the moment that Jesus shares He is Christ, that He needed to go to the place where the 'undesirable,' lesser perceived people dwelled. Jesus' actions remind us of our true spiritual nature and loving relationship with God. In what ways have you felt rejected or disregarded? How does it feel to know that Jesus seeks you out? Jesus sees, knows, and loves you exactly as you are.

Jesus set out on His journey to Samaria long before the Samaritan woman began her walk to the well. This is a metaphor for our lives. Jesus/God has divine appointments with us and sets the wheels in motion for those divine arrangements long before we even get the inclination in our spirit to go to a place, or do something. God knows ahead of time and divinely aligns the highest path for our journey and the greater good. This meeting between Jesus and the Samaritan woman wasn't just to bless and transform her, but also for those lives she would impact in sharing the message of the Messiah and the way we would learn to shift our acceptance of others and how we embrace Jesus' message of worshipping in Spirit and truth. Just as this passage is layered with learnings and blessings, so, too, is the tapestry of our own lives and the lives of all.

God is paving a way for us, even when we dwell in an undesirable place, have made mistakes in life, or are seen as lesser than others in our environment. God has our divine appointments in place. If ever you feel despair, overwhelmed, or uncertain of which way to turn in life, remind yourself of the Samaritan woman, readying herself to collect water at the well, unknowing of the divinely arranged appointment with Jesus and how her life would transform when she chose to worship in Spirit and truth (John 4:24, NKJV).

Siobhan B.

In John 4, Jesus exemplifies how sometimes, the route we need to take in life on our journey with God isn't always going to be the most convenient or approved of route. Jesus shows us that walking a journey of worship in Spirit and truth (John 4:24, NKJV) with God, prevails above limitations of what other people say, do, or expect of us. I remember the moment I found out I was pregnant. I knew in my spirit that I had to have this baby and that all would align perfectly for us; that God had blessed me with this miracle and I must trust that it will work out well. I was fearful of how others would react, what they would say, and how much my life would change—becoming a single mother, no longer being able to continue the jobs I was doing at that time. I remembered how all my life, I believed I would either be a 'much older mum' or wouldn't have children at all and yet there I was, knowing deep within that I was meant to have this baby and it would be my greatest challenge and blessing. Having my daughter has been the most challenging and blessed part of my journey to date. I am forever grateful that God knew this less approved of, less accepted, totally unexpected path was the one that would bring forth so much of the greatness within me that's needed to fulfill my calling in this lifetime.

Have you ever felt moved in your spirit to action, something that others believed you weren't worthy of? Have you ever allowed fear to get in the way of actioning a dream or reaching out to people/a loved one? I remember years ago when I began training in various coaching techniques and people would say to me that I was too young, or they didn't believe I would really do much with the qualifications. Now, thirteen years later, I look back and I know the great impact I have already made and what transformation has taken place within me throughout this journey—now, those naysayers praise the fruits of my work, the fruits that I had sensed in my spirit when all I had was the roots. Allow yourself to trust in the path that God calls you to walk. Trust in the route your spirit calls you to take in alignment with God.

Others may not understand or praise until your tree of prosperity is laden with fruits. Worry not, for they are not given your vision. Your assignment is truly between you and God.

The Well

The use of water—just as in Genesis 1.

"In the beginning God created the heavens and the earth. The earth was without form, and void; and darkness was on the face of the deep. And the Spirit of God was hovering over the face of the waters" (Genesis 1:1-2, NKJV).

At the beginning of time, there was water (the deep is also water) and now in John 4 when Jesus reveals that He is Christ, He uses water as a metaphor. The symbolism of the Well and the water is divinely arranged, again enhancing the significance of this meeting of the Samaritan woman and Jesus at the well. I also feel this symbolism of water represents a new beginning in our worship with God, as Jesus shares the way in which we all must worship, which is not only for the Jews and no longer about being of one particular group.

Jesus said to her, *"Woman, believe Me, the hour is coming when you will neither on this mountain, nor in Jerusalem, worship the Father. You worship what you do not know; we know what we worship, for salvation is of the Jews. But the hour is coming, and now is, when the true worshipers will worship the Father in spirit and truth; for the Father is seeking such to worship Him. God is Spirit, and those who worship Him must worship in spirit and truth"* (John 4:21-24, NKJV).

Jesus is sharing in the moment that He tells He is the Messiah, that *"God is Spirit, and those who worship Him must worship in Spirit and truth"* (John 4:24, NKJV). This is the message that Jesus wants us to carry with us above all in John 4. Jesus shares that *"the hour is coming, and now is, when the true worshipers will worship the Father in Spirit and truth; for the Father is seeking such to worship Him"* (John 4:23, NKJV). We learn the hour is coming, and now is and it is not about the person's race, gender, sins of the past, or social status/group—but the way they worship.

The Well and symbolism of water is further utilized in John 4 to represent our needs. We as humans, are mostly made up of water and thirst for water, that which we are. Likewise, God is Spirit, and those who worship Him must worship in Spirit and truth (John 4:24, NKJV). We are told that the Father is seeking such to worship Him (John 4:23, NKJV). It is so rare to hear that God is seeking something. Often, we are led to believe that God is, has, and does all things—yet here we learn that God seeks, 'thirsts,' for us to worship Him in Spirit—this is the message Jesus wanted us to know when He revealed He is the Messiah. Jesus wanted us to know that God wants and seeks us, just as we want and seek to be close to God in our spirits. How blessed we are that God seeks each and every one of us.

Jesus chose to rest at the Well. How beautiful it is that God meets us at our place of human need. The need for water is universal in all humans regardless of our status, gender, race, or religion. Here is where Jesus chose to meet the Samaritan Woman and share that He is Christ.

I am Her... the Woman at the Well

"Jesus, therefore, being wearied from His journey, sat thus by the well" (John 4:6, NKJV). Here, we are reminded of Jesus' humanity. He was wearied from His journey, much as we can often become wearied from our journeys in life, and in our time of weariness is when we tend to most seek after 'wells' to quench our thirst. Jesus speaks of living water and tells the Samaritan woman of this well where she collects water:

"Jesus answered and said to her, "Whoever drinks of this water will thirst again, but whoever drinks of the water that I shall give him will never thirst. But the water that I shall give him will become in him a fountain of water springing up into everlasting life" (John 4:13-14, NKJV).

Here, Jesus is talking of a spiritual well, God as our source, the Living Water that is everlasting for each and every one of us. Jesus uses the water as a metaphor to show us a physical well of water that leaves us thirsting and seeking, compared to the spiritual water from God that when we receive it, it becomes a fountain of water springing up into everlasting life (John 4:14, NKJV). So often, when we attempt to meet our needs with physical things, we go to wells that leave us thirsting for more.

Whether it is alcohol, substances, sexual gratification, food, attention, achievement, or any of the other numerous human wells at which we can temporarily meet a need that will again leave us thirsting. The physical world well is a metaphor for the temporary fix which leaves us needing for more without realizing that well was covering up a much deeper need within us. That need is met and fulfilled with a fountain of water springing up into everlasting life, (John 4:14, NKJV) when we go to the spiritual well of our source, God.

I truly believe that if the Samaritan woman had known her full worth, she wouldn't have had five husbands, and the one that she was currently with in the scripture who was not her husband (John 4:18, NKJV). If she had gone to God's fountain, she would have chosen differently and experienced a different path. I can certainly relate to having been in relationships, trying to meet a deep need to feel loved and feel worthy, seeking physical wells that always left me dependent on returning to quench a thirst that could only be truly met through the spiritual understanding of my worthiness and relationship with God.

I am reminded of Colossians 3:2, NKJV where it says to *"set your mind on things above, not on things on the earth."* What physical world wells have you sought after in your life? Can you notice now how these physical world wells left you thirsting for more and never truly honored your worthiness, or met that spiritual need deep within you? How does it feel to know that the Father is seeking (John 4:23, NKJV) you? Speak with God. Pray. Ask for assistance as you worship in Spirit and truth (John 4:24, NKJV) and release any physical wells you had once thirst after.

In Truth

Often, when the truth of our lives, including our sins, mistakes, and shame are witnessed in the presence of love, the weight is lifted from us and we remember our true nature.

The woman then left her waterpot, went her way into the city, and said to the men, *"Come, see a Man who told me all things that I ever did. Could this be the Christ? Then, they went out of the city and came to Him"* (John 4:28-30, NKJV).

The Samaritan woman did not take to the streets to exclaim that Jesus spoke of an everlasting spiritual well, she talked of how He knew her—all things that I ever did (John 4:29, NKJV). Have you ever been in the presence of a friend, soul-sister, or one that you deeply trust and when you share a truth about yourself that you'd hidden or felt ashamed of, as you see them accept and love you, the weight and shame is lifted or eased? Now imagine/remember how much deeper and more powerful that is when we turn to Jesus/God to share our truth and be witnessed by Him with unconditional love.

God knows us, all of us, and all we have done. God is our witness and still loves us. Through reading and praying over this passage, I have taken time with God to speak about all the ways that I have judged and condemned myself. The parts I hid or felt ashamed of. The choices that I've wanted to hide from the world. Yet, as I speak with God and study John 4, I learn that our mistakes, or the ways we become lost, are not a condition that cuts us off from God's grace and love. Instead, it is through the acceptance, releasing of shame, and growing beyond condemnation or separation consciousness that we can walk in truth and Spirit with our Source.

The Samaritan woman was seen and accepted, not judged or disregarded by Jesus upon Jesus speaking her truth to her and sharing that the true worshipers will worship the Father in Spirit and truth; for the Father is seeking such to worship Him. God is Spirit, and those who worship Him must worship in Spirit and truth (John 4:23-24, NKJV). It's almost as if the woman's spirit was freed to go to the city and share of the Messiah with the people.

Siobhan B.

As a Samaritan woman who *"had five husbands, and the one whom you now have is not your husband,"* (John 4:18, NKJV) she would have been an outcast of society and her attending the well at noon, a time when others would usually not be there as they would have gone early morning or late evening, is another indication that she hid away in shame and condemnation, which she was freed from when she was witnessed in her truth and spoke from her spirit, the word of the Messiah.

How would you speak, walk, and share God's message differently if you knew you were loved beyond any mistake or sin you have made? How would your life transform if you chose to speak with God in truth about all you have done and worship from your spirit, knowing you need not hide parts of yourself any longer? What courage will you feel when you share your encounters with Christ and free yourself from the condemnation/separation of others?

A Mirror

Jesus said to her, *"Go, call your husband, and come here."* The woman answered and said, *"I have no husband."* Jesus said to her, *"You have well said, 'I have no husband,' for you have had five husbands, and the one whom you now have is not your husband; in that you spoke truly."* The woman said to Him, *"Sir, I perceive that You are a prophet. Our fathers worshiped on this mountain, and you Jews say that in Jerusalem is the place where one ought to worship"* (John 4:16-20, NKJV).

When Jesus reflected back to the Samaritan woman, her truth—she attempts to deflect the attention away and onto another subject. Much like in life, when we feel sin or shame, we can try to distract or deflect from those things. Yet, in John 4, we see how by Jesus being a mirror to the woman's truth without any judgement, just unconditional love and presence, the woman is then liberated and freed from the weight of her self-condemnation.

The Samaritan woman had gone to the well at 12 noon, it's clearly indicated through these details that the woman's shame and sin of having many husbands/partners has separated her from the other women and people of the city. When in your life have you felt lesser than other women or disconnected from the feeling of sisterhood? How has this disconnection from fellow sisters impacted your life, spirit, and self-worth? When Jesus witnesses her and reflects back her truth without shaming or condemning her, just acknowledging her truthfulness, she is changed. Later in John 4 we read:

"The woman left her waterpot, went her way into the city, and said to the men, Come, see a Man who told me all things that I ever did. Could this be the Christ?" Then they went out of the city and came to Him" (John 4:28-30, NKJV).

Notice how she speaks of *"all things that I ever did,"* (John 4:29, NKJV) and she is going to the city and speaking to the people, not hiding away and separating herself. That which had once cut her off from people now connected her through worship[ping] in Spirit and truth (John 4:24, NKJV).

Much like Jesus did with the Samaritan woman, when we look at ourselves in the mirror and see what is reflected, when we witness our 'truth' with presence and unconditional love (rather than criticism or self-judgement), we are able to live in our truth and step into our highest calling in life. Often, self-judgement and condemnation leave us feeling isolated, unworthy, separate from others and then as a result, we can end up choosing actions (like visiting the well at noon) which further isolate and add to the shame/toxic cycle. How differently would you see yourself if you could look in the mirror without judging or criticizing yourself, but instead witness your truth with unconditional love? As women, we can be so conditioned to feel 'not good enough'—the Samaritan woman, even with all her flaws was not only 'good enough,' but was chosen. You, too, are worthy, seen in all of your truth and loved unconditionally by God.

How often have you tried to distract others from noticing your perceived flaws or mistakes? Where in your life have you judged yourself and then through the tinge of judgement, shifted your actions, choices, and beliefs about what's possible for you?

On My Knees
I am reminded of the times that I dropped to my knees on my kitchen or sitting room floor (usually those are the places), alone at night in solitude in times of great challenge, where I find myself on my knees with my face to the ground crying out to God for guidance. At the points when the physical world 'well' I used to quench thirsts that were cover ups for the ways in which I had forgotten or abandoned my true spirit. The times when I reached points that I could not continue to superficially pacify the thirst of my soul to reconnect with God—that's when I would give in and drop to my knees asking for help. The times when I had the courage to cry out all the things I wish I hadn't done, the mistakes, fear, and anger that had pulled me from my true loving essence.

I am Her... the Woman at the Well

In those moments when I prayed and worship[ped] in Spirit and truth (John 4:24, NKJV) is when I could hear and feel God speaking back to me, guiding and loving me beyond any mistake or shame. Each time I went back to the well of God, I found a fountain of water springing up into everlasting life (John 4:14, NKJV). God would always hear me.

Allow me to feel His ever-loving omniscience and omnipresence. Only when I sought after physical world thirsts that have not been true to my spirit and the source from which I came, have I found myself thirsting and returning to wells that can never quench me, as they are not of living water (John 4:10, NKJV).

Where in your life have you sought to quench thirsts through physical world wells? Do you remember how each trip back to those worldly wells pacified your thirst but never sprung a source of everlasting water for you, too?

When we shift our focus to being, living, and worshiping in Spirit and truth, no longer focusing on the flesh or worldly matters, we are released of all mistakes from our past. You are never too far down the path of mistakes/sins to be loved by God. You are never unworthy. Your choosing to walk in Spirit and truth, to connect with God and realign your thoughts, actions, and intentions with the Source from which you came, will set you on the right path. It is never too late.

"There is therefore now no condemnation to those who are in Christ Jesus, who do not walk according to the flesh, but according to the Spirit" (Romans 8:1, NKJV).

Allow yourself to release the weights of self-condemnation. Pray and journal with God. Open up to worshipping in Spirit and truth. Allow your true worthiness to shine through. God sees all things, you are never too late, forgotten, or beyond loving.

Service Not Glory

Jesus spoke with the Samaritan woman having sent the disciples away to get food and yet when they return, He says He has no need for food. Here, we come to understand even deeper that this meeting of Jesus with the Samaritan woman was not about displaying or showing off to others. It was not about reflecting the woman's truth of her multiple husbands in front of the disciples, which could have added to her feeling of shame or condemnation. It was about Jesus' meeting with her, one-on-one, something so unheard of for those times/societies and reflecting to the Samaritan woman the spiritual well of God that is available for her, too.

This gracious act by Jesus reminds us of the importance of serving in Spirit and not for glory. Much as we are told *"take heed that you do not do your charitable deeds before men, to be seen by them. Otherwise, you have no reward from your Father in heaven"* (Matthew 6:1, NKJV). God truly wants us to worship and serve in Spirit and truth (John 4:23-24, NKJV) and not for physical world approval, or glory. Just as Jesus waited for His divine appointment alone with the Samaritan woman, to share this deeply layered message as He confirmed that He is the Messiah, rather than confirming He is the Messiah when He was with Nicodemus in John 3.

Uncomfortable

Studying this passage has been such a blessing and equally so very uncomfortable. I have faced so many truths about myself and my journey. I have taken the time to consider each well in my life. Intimate relationships/partners, eating, achievements/successes, self-judgement, and condemnation, the need to feel and be loved, the use of substances, admiration, rebellion, anger, and so much more. Each one has been a way in which I was attempting to meet a deep need within myself, but the need was only met at the surface level and therefore left me thirsting shortly after. As I dive into understanding each of those needs, it is clear that the need was there because at some point, I had forgotten the true essence of my spirit and the God Source from which I came. I had looked to a physical world well instead of God. In John 4, Jesus reminds us that as we worship God fully with our spirits, truthfully and honestly —all our thirsts are quenched by a well that never runs dry. God is our source for all needs—having a need merely indicates that we are 'in need' of connecting more and deeper with our Spiritual Source.

Where in life have you thirst? What wells have you sought to pacify your Spiritual needs? How can you commit now to speak, pray, and sit with Jesus/God at that well of your need and be witnessed in your truth, fully with unconditional love? God seeks you. You are loved and fully accepted and embraced as you are. There is an everlasting well that is waiting for you to come to it in Spirit and truth. All you need to do is turn to God instead of physical world wells.

Wearied by Life

Having studied this text deeper, I am glad the Samaritan woman isn't given a name as on some level, I would have felt she is separate from, special, or different to me in some way. *I am her*, she is me. She is each of us that have felt rejected, judged, condemned, lived in shame, or forgotten the greatness of our true spirits and the source from which we came.

I pray that you remember and walk in your greatness with God. I pray that you release yourself from self-condemnation and go to the spiritual well of Jesus' unconditional, ever-lasting love that sees and knows you fully. Jesus seeks you out. He goes to the places that others judge or avoid. He is waiting at the well for you—you have a divine appointment together. Jesus understands the human journey and that we can all become 'wearied' and shows us that in those moments of weariness, we need not turn to the physical temporary quenching of thirst, but instead go to the spiritual well that is ever-lasting. The God from which we came.

You are Worthy

"In the meantime His disciples urged Him, saying, "Rabbi, eat." But He said to them, "I have food to eat of which you do not know." Therefore the disciples said to one another, "Has anyone brought Him anything to eat?" (John 4:31-33, NKJV).

Even the disciples who traveled with Jesus had yet to fully understand the new way to worship and the spiritual well where God meets all our needs. In the section above, we are reminded that even when people are well versed in God/Jesus' Word, they can still be distracted by physical world needs. Their position does not mean that they worship in a 'better' way than you. You need not hold back because others can quote scripture or have been on a journey with God or attending a church longer than you. I knew of John 4 decades ago and yet only through studying and living with this text these last few months has my insight with the passage and the Samaritan woman deepened. Your worship in Spirit and truth (John 4:24, NKJV) with God is what matters.

Through Your Testimony

"And many of the Samaritans of that city believed in Him because of the word of the woman who testified, "He told me all that I ever did." So, when the Samaritans had come to Him, they urged Him to stay with them; and He stayed there two days. And many more believed because of His own word. Then they said to the woman, "Now we believe, not because of what you said, for we ourselves have heard Him and we know that this is indeed the Christ, the Savior of the world." (John 4:39-42, NKJV).

You do not know the ripple effect you can create, the difference you can make. The Samaritan woman went from avoiding the people of the city to being a messenger that helped them transform their lives as well as her own. As she stepped into her truth and spiritual fullness, her life transformed and people's perceptions of her transformed in turn. You need not wait for others to approve of you. When you worship in Spirit and truth (John 4:24, NKJV), you will find courage and take actions that may currently feel beyond your ability. Focus now on your relationship with God. Share your truth, your pains, or your fears and listen to God's answers. Ask for guidance when facing a challenge. Sit to meditate, journal, pray, or sing. Allow yourself to find the way that works best for you, so you can open up to the spiritual well that awaits you.

Imagine

Imagine how your life will transform if you sit with and pray over the wisdom shared in John 4. Open up to the possibility that Jesus has divine appointments with you, too. That regardless of how you have lived up until this moment, God seeks to connect with you in Spirit and truth. Your whole truth. Jesus chose to share that He is Christ with someone of a different race, gender, and religion and someone who was deemed to be living in great sin—His love stretched beyond lines of separation bringing forth unconditional love and unity consciousness in all that He did. Jesus paved the way for a new perspective on our relationship with God and how we are meant to worship. Take the time to pray, journal, and sit at the well of the thirsts in your life—those needs you have tried to quench through physical world wells. Reflect without judgement. Be open to connecting with God in Spirit and truth for your thirst to be met spiritually by an everlasting fountain. You are never beyond help, or love. There may even be a city of people that had once judged you, whose lives you will help transform, as you remember your true spiritual essence.

Connect with Siobhan B.:
  Email: siobhan@siobhanb.com
  Website: www.siobhanb.com
  LinkedIn: www.linkedin.com/in/siobhanbcoach/
  Instagram: @siobhanbcoach
  Facebook: @siobhanbcoach
  YouTube: www.youtube.com/siobhanbcoach
  TikTok: @siobhanbcoach

Ponder *I am Her*... Strings of Wisdom for reflection:

_____
_____
_____
_____
_____
_____
_____
_____
_____
_____
_____
_____
_____
_____
_____
_____
_____
_____
_____
_____
_____
_____
_____
_____
_____
_____
_____

Chapter Twelve

I am Her... Mary, called Magdalene

Barbara Saunders

I am The Witness

*N*ow Mary stood outside the tomb crying. As she wept, she bent over to look into the tomb and saw two angels in white, seated where Jesus' body had been, one at the head and the other at the foot. They asked her, "Woman, why are you crying?"

"They have taken my Lord away," she said, "and I don't know where they have put him." At this, she turned around and saw Jesus standing there, but she did not realize that it was Jesus. He asked her, "Woman, why are you crying? Who is it you are looking for?" Thinking he was the gardener, she said, "Sir, if you have carried him away, tell me where you have put him, and I will get him." Jesus said to her, "Mary." She turned toward him and cried out in Aramaic, "Rabboni!" (which means "Teacher"). Jesus said, "Do not hold on to me, for I have not yet ascended to the Father. Go instead to my brothers and tell them, 'I am ascending to my Father and your Father, to my God and your God.'" Mary Magdalene went to the disciples with the news:

Barbara Saunders

"I have seen the Lord!" And she told them that he had said these things to her" (John 20:11-18, NIV).

Everyone likes a juicy story, and although most people hold on to the notion that they do not gossip, when you start off your sentence with "Girrrrl, let me tell you," it's gossip. "Dude, did you know…" it's gossip. "I don't tell other people's business, but…" —it's gossip. We have even turned sharing a cup of tea into a listening party with the saying *spill the tea.* We are so engrossed in telling someone else's story and so I invite you to take a walk with me and embark upon the journey of Mary Magdalene whose life's experiences are ours even today…

Who is Mary Magdalene you may wonder? Well, I believe Mary is a woman no different than each of us. A woman who wears many hats and carries many titles. A woman full of great talent yet shamed by the haters. When she loved, she loved hard. When she worked, she worked until her feet hurt. When she befriended you, she gave all of who she was even to her detriment. Like so many women, Mary knew there was something deep inside, a yearning to be free, a longing for the fulfillment that only true love could satisfy. Who is Mary Magdalene you may wonder? Mary is you. Mary is me. Mary is every woman.

As a child, I recall having a recurring dream. This dream would haunt me for a few years, replaying in my world of sleep as though it was on repeat. In this dream, I would be at the end of a long underground parking garage and a woman who appeared to be my mother would be squatting at the opposite end with her arms open wide. To paint this picture a bit more vividly, I seemed to be inside the garage, where it was dark and my mother was calling for me at the opening of the parking lot, on the outside. Had I wandered so far away that I was in darkness? In my dream, I was always so excited to hear that voice calling out to me, letting me know to change direction and look toward the light. I anticipated the jump into the arms of safety, so I would take off running.

As soon as I was close enough to know for certain it was my mom, the lot would grow longer and longer as though I would never reach her. My mom's face would suddenly grow blank and I realized the yearning desire to be in my mother's arms would never happen. The scene would eventually fade and then the dream would be over. I would awaken in a daze, confused and honestly, mad as hell not understanding what just happened. What was this dream all about? You see, I did not grow up with my biological mother. I was adopted. And every single memory I have of her, I am unable to see her face. Did I say I would wake up mad as hell, even as a child? Well, I am still annoyed that I have NO RECOLLECTION of my mother's face. Those that knew her have said all I have to do is look in the mirror, but that does me no good. I have never seen Mae Shirley. I have only seen Barbara Louise. As I stated previously, this dream used to haunt me. It became one full of disappointment because even in my dreams, I could not find the peace I longed for, my mother.

The internal struggles we encounter become the demons that taunt us, haunt us, and try to turn our world inside out. This dream played tricks with my mind and caused turmoil within. Have you ever felt you were wrestling with yourself? So often, we think of casting out demons as solely "ghostly spirits" that invade our bodies. Let me be clear, demonic forces are definitely real and have made themselves at home in many people. But have we ever considered that the demons within can also be those sins which weigh us down, entrap us, or hold us back?

When we first meet Mary Magdalene, we learn that she had been in the company of Jesus, who cast out of her seven demons. Luke 8:2 (NIV) says, *"... and also some women who had been cured of evil spirits and diseases: Mary (called Magdalene) from whom seven demons had come out."* What an introduction! Deception, darkness, temptation, and a life of continual torment was Mary's path before meeting Jesus. Demonic possession controlled her personality and led to voices speaking through the person, fits, and acts of unusual power. My curious mind wants to know what specific demons did Jesus cast out, and what was Mary running from. Does that really matter to tell her story? It is of no relevance. And if I am going to gain anything from her, I must be honest, and really ask myself, what demons am I running from? What, if anything, are you running from?

The epiphany of my dream revealed to me that so often, we struggle with internal chaos, demons that keep us running from truth. In all that Mary encountered, she finally stopped running from whatever were her infirmities and ran to the One who could redeem her. When I realized the One whose arms could provide me the comfort and love I so desperately desired and longed for, I stopped running from my reality. And truth be told, I still have my moments of despair when those *why me Lord* moments try to take me back down a rabbit hole from which I have already been rescued. When I begin to get in my own way, I am reminded that while I will always be a motherless child, I will NEVER be fatherless.

Jesus delivered Mary from her demonic condition. And just like that, she went from being ostracized to being set free. In gratitude, she became a faithful follower and disciple. And life would never be the same again. Talk about being at the right place at the right time. She encountered the One who traveled from town to town, village to village, healing those who desired healing and teaching a new way of life. When I think about her healing, I realize that only a Savior can deliver us from such strongholds. Strongholds are lies that become our normal, our truth. Strongholds become something that we run to for comfort when we are stressed and afraid. They begin to shape us. We become our strongholds. We begin to look like what we worship either for our good or for our destruction. 2 Corinthians 10:4,5 (NIV) states, *"The weapons we fight with are not the weapons of the world. On the contrary, they have divine power to demolish strongholds. We demolish arguments and every pretension that sets itself up against the knowledge of God, and we take captive every thought to make it obedient to Christ."*

Growing up was challenging for me. Not because I was unloved, although I have struggled all my life with that four letter word "love" and how vastly different it is expressed, but because I was a constant reminder of my past, my origin. I did not know my biological mother to remember her. I remember events that have shaped me. However, others around me continued to plant the seed of how I would probably be *just like her*. I took offense to those words. You see, Mae Shirley, which was my mother's name, did not live to see beyond the age of thirty or so. Unfortunately, street life became her demonic stronghold and she left two children in a world that would teach them more than either wanted to experience.

While I can look back at my life now and know it is the grace of God that covered me, the decisions I made along the way were survival driven. When you are trying to make sense of what does not make sense and hold on when you have no one to hold on to, survival mode kicks in. Your mind and body become focused on combating danger. And when you sense danger is near, that barrier is formed and you cannot see beyond it. I kept many people out who genuinely loved me for fear of being abandoned again. But I experienced many perpetrators along the way who meant no good. You see, the enemy tries to invade your life through lies that he plants in your brain. If you do not take your thoughts captive, it will be just a matter of time before those demons start using the lies to create mental and emotional strongholds that will keep you in bondage. But just like Mary, Jesus delivered me and has set the captive free. I am no longer bound by the lies planted inside me. And even though life was void of my mother's love, I can boldly declare Psalm 139:14 which says, *"For you formed my inward parts; you knitted me together in my mother's womb. I praise you, for I am fearfully and wonderfully made."*

To be able to sit at the feet of Jesus and witness miracle after miracle, soaking up the knowledge of His teachings, was mesmerizing and Mary grew a love for the Teacher that was indescribable. You know that kind of love, that tingling feeling you get when the relationship is fresh and new and you cannot stop smiling, giggling, gazing, and thinking about them. Every waking moment, you are counting the hours to be back in each other's presence. That innocent kind of love that has you on a high as you learn more and more about each other. Jesus is probably the first man who did not condemn Mary for her past. After all, she had a reputation. Even the disciples identified her as Mary of seven demons! This act of love to follow Jesus and support the ministry out of her own means was the least she could do for her freedom, for He showed her how to live and how to love. The necessity to show people love, and love in return, is paramount. What she would later learn is the One who did not condemn her would be the One to take her place, your place, and my place as the condemned. What do you do when the warmth of love suddenly turns to grief?

There are some who believe tears are a waste and cannot solve anything, but I beg to differ. The purging that one experiences from releasing whatever is bottled up inside becomes therapy. Tears have always been my liquid therapy. Now, I can agree it may not solve the issue at hand but it sure becomes a relax, relate, and release moment that is therapeutically healing. It cleanses my soul, so I can allow the Holy Spirit to work.

Jesus spoke in the prophetic to the disciples about what would happen, but it had not become real to any of them and in all honesty, His message seemed so conflicting. No one could grasp what was to come. The day that would change our lives forever was finally upon them and all hell broke loose, literally. Jesus' ministry seemed to end abruptly, in the blink of an eye. Those against Him were operating under the sole direction of the enemy and Jesus was arrested, falsely accused, beaten inhumanely, and ultimately crucified. Mary and the other women followers witnessed the entire ordeal as they had more freedom to move about and were not under the cloud of suspicion by the spectators as the male disciples, who, by the way, were very afraid for their own lives.

Mary, however, had the courage to see her discipleship to the very end. Truly she was a *ride or die* kind of girl. Can you imagine being with Jesus, knowing the miracles, seeing the miracles, being a miracle, and longing in this moment of despair for the Master to perform one last miracle and save Himself! Jesus is in agony and so are those who loved Him, who watched this horrific crucifixion. Mary would quickly have to rely on the teachings of the Master to give her strength. She was in a place called Golgotha. A place of suffering. A place of punishment. A place of sacrifice. Mary had come full circle being cleansed of demons only to witness Jesus being crucified at a place where demonic behavior abounds.

Once Jesus took His last breath and declared, *'It is finished,'* Mary's grief became profound. What was she to do without Jesus? The One who had raised the dead is now dead. Death seems so permanent to us since Christ has not yet returned for His children. I can only imagine the knot in her throat and in the pit of her stomach as the Sabbath approaches and she is forced to rest. She had to leave Jesus at the tomb and wait. She lamented over her Savior and the thought she would never be with Him again left her devastated and in unspeakable pain.

I have been to many funerals in my life. In fact, I remember my very first funeral. It was my grandfather's. I believe I was no older than five. As it turns out, my biological mother was also adopted. Just to give you a glimpse of background history, her adoptive parents were named Charles and Barbara. How coincidental that me and my brother are named Barbara and Charles. Anyway, when street life became Mae Shirley's addiction, I was often left with my grandpa Charles. When he died, I stood at his casket for a long time. I was told he was sleeping, so I asked what any child would ask, "When is he going to wake up because I need to talk to him." Needless to say, he never woke up and once again, I was abandoned.

Feelings of abandonment can have a great effect on your mental state and for me, it has carried over into my adulthood. The feeling of drawing close only to lose someone has caused me to be very guarded. When I love, I love hard but when I cut it off, it is as though love was never there. This defense mechanism aims at protecting my heart but does not leave room for grace. Lord, change me! Thank God for Jesus who is the repairer of the breach, mending these broken pieces of my heart and tearing down the walls. God assures He has not abandoned me. God has not abandoned you. When we lay it all down at the Cross, we find redemption. Hebrews 12:1 (KJV) states, *"Therefore, seeing we also are compassed about by so great a cloud of witnesses, let us lay aside every weight, and the sin which doth so easily beset us, and let us run with patience the race that is set before us."*

Mary was determined to lay her eyes on Jesus again, so early in the morning after the Sabbath ended, she headed to the tomb where He was buried. Much to her surprise, she finds the opening of the tomb unsealed and no Jesus. OMG! Are you kidding me? Talk about being an emotional wreck. I can undoubtedly say Mary wrestled all night with little to no sleep, replaying in her mind over and over what had just happened. How is it that in less than 24 hours, Jesus is gone. Frantic and almost at her wits end, she sees two angels seated where Jesus' body was laid yet doesn't even realize she is in the presence of ANGELS. When you are on a mission with tunnel vision, you see nothing.

Shortly after her encounter with the angels, she sees Jesus yet doesn't realize who He is. It is not until He calls her by name that she recognizes hope has been restored. Jesus is, in fact, the risen Savior. She reaches out to embrace her Teacher but cannot as He has not yet ascended to the Father in Heaven. He does, however, leave her with an important message to relay and gladly, she goes to deliver the word spoken by Jesus to the other disciples. I am blown away at the fact Jesus waited for Mary before ascending to the Father. Let's be honest with ourselves. Of all the people in the circle, Mary is the chosen one. The very first to proclaim that Christ has risen.

Sorrow has immediately turned to joy. Mary remembered the prediction of Jesus' death and in that moment, the light came on and she understood what it all meant. What an honor to be the first person to truly interpret the resurrection. You see, when you are on this Christ walk, you realize when life happens, you don't always have it figured out. The chaos, the chatter, the noise needs to be quieted. The approach to simplify things just a bit, takes on a new meaning. Mary is reminded of these words, *"I'm telling you these things while I'm still living with you. The Friend, the Holy Spirit whom the Father will send at my request, will make everything plain to you. He will remind you of all the things I have told you. I'm leaving you well and whole. That's my parting gift to you. Peace. I don't leave you the way you're used to being left—feeling abandoned, bereft. So don't be upset. Don't be distraught"* (John 14:25-27, MSG).

I have been baptized twice, first at sixteen and the second time at twenty-five. The nine years in between, I found myself slipping into the abyss of despair. Those were the most challenging years of my life and the loneliest years of my life. The enemy was doing his best to prove the naysayers right that I would be just like 'my mother'. But the devil is a liar and there is no truth in him. And while I made some of the most foolish mistakes, missed so many opportunities, two things happened during the nine years that changed my life forever: the birth of my son at age twenty-two and the rededication of my life to the Lord at twenty-five. I urge you to not allow the demons, the strongholds, or the sins in your life to block your blessings and keep you enslaved. The struggles you face are real and you will have to endure the gut punches of life. But be encouraged that even at your lowest, God's got you. God fights our battles and God wins.

The one full of seven demons, became Jesus' witness. He trusted her by revealing Himself fully, even before ascending to His Father in Heaven and waited for her arrival because He knew she was loyal, she was faithful, and she loved Him to the end. The one full of seven demons becomes one of the most important people in the entire New Testament. What a privilege God bestowed upon Mary. The eyes of humanity saw Mary as an outcast; a woman demonized, a woman rejected, a woman stigmatized. The eyes of Jesus saw Mary as an apostle; a woman forgiven; a woman uplifted, a woman transformed.

We are all living testaments of God's mighty power and ultimate love. He uses ordinary people to perform miracles, and restores what has been damaged, what has been destroyed. God used *Eve* to bring forth life. He reminds us through Lot's wife to stay the course and not look back. God used *Leah* for His glory despite her feeling unloved by man. *Miriam* is our example of how words matter. God used *Rahab* to prove no one can serve two masters. *Deborah* teaches us that devotion to God leads to victory. God used *Abigail* to show us that there is power in humility. *The Proverbs 31 Woman* teaches us the character of God isn't all about doing, it's everything about becoming. God used *The Woman Healed on the Sabbath* to teach us that deliverance is available for all with no restrictions. The parable of *The Persistent Widow* simply teaches us to pray without ceasing and never give up. God used *The Woman at the Well* to teach us that only He can quench the thirst of our souls.

What will your story be for all to witness? Get that cup ready my sisters, it is time to spill the tea!

I have seen the Lord: *I am Mary (called Magdalene)*, the one whom Jesus cast out seven demons and I am The Witness. *I AM HER!*

Connect with Barbara Saunders:

Email: BarbaraLouSaunders@gmail.com or blraqi@icloud.com.

Ponder *I am Her*... Strings of Wisdom for reflection:

Meet the Author
Nycholle Woolfolk-Gater

Nycholle Woolfolk-Gater is a passionate God-fearing woman who spends her time seeking ways to lead the masses to Christ. As a *Soldier Family Readiness Specialist*, she works to strengthen the military family and veterans. She is a *Certified Master Resiliency Trainer* and *Certified Life Coach* providing Marriage and Relationship Coaching to couples and Fine Tune the Vision Coaching for individuals.

Nycholle is married to Darrick E. Gater, and they share four children together: Brittany, Amber, Colby, and Devin, and two son-in-loves: Eugene and Benjamin, along with four grandchildren: Kingston, Tristan, Tessa, and Teagan.

Nycholle is the author of four books, "Dry Bones, God's Plan for Restoring Marriage," "Dry Bones the Journal from Reconstruction to Restoration," "The Promises in "I Do," a 31-Day Marriage Devotional" and "Real Conversations for Couples Before the Rings," all available on her website and Amazon.

Nycholle is available for individual or couple coaching. If you would like to have Nycholle speak to your women's ministry, marriage group, or to facilitate a workshop, she can be reached online at www.nwgllc.com.